STEEPLE ENVY
by Victor Cuccia

Published by

THINK

All Scripture quotations, unless otherwise noted, are taken from the *Holy Bible, New International Version*. NIV. Copyright 1973, 1978, 1984 by International Bible Society. Used by permission of Zondervan. All rights reserved.

Scripture quotations marked ESV are taken from *The Holy Bible English Standard Version*. Copyright 2000; 2001 by Crossway Bibles, a division of Good News Publishers. Used by permission.

Scripture quotations marked *The Message Bible* are taken from THE MESSAGE. Copyright © 1993, 1994, 1995, 1996, 2000, 2001, 2002. Used by permission of NavPress Publishing Group.

Scripture quotations marked NLT are taken from the Holy Bible, New Living Translation, copyright 1996, 2004. Used by permission of Tyndale House Publishers, Inc., Wheaton Illinois. All rights reserved.

Scripture quotations marked CEV are from the Contemporary English Version Copyright © 1991, 1992, 1995 by American Bible Society, Used by Permission.

Italics in Scripture quotations have been added by the author for emphasis.

ISBN 978-0-615-50992-1

Victor Cuccia

Cover Design: Mike Henin
Interior Layout: Renuka Christoph

Author Photo: Kate Barnette

Printed in the United States of America
First Edition 2011

INSPIRATION:

Thank you to those who have inspired me along my journey:

Rob Bell, Francis Chan, Donald Miller, Mark Driscoll, David Platt, A.W. Tozer, Hugh Halter, Matt Smay, Alan Hirsch, U2, Michael Knott, R.E.M, Switchfoot, P.O.D, Vigilantes of Love, Andrew Petersen and Bob Dylan.

eNCOURAGEMENT:

Thank you to everyone who has encouraged me and helped make this book a reality:

Sherrie Clark for all your hard work in making it readable; Mike Henin for the killer art work; Kate Barnett for the pics; Renuka Christoph for the pagination, which added a new word to my vocabulary; Brock Johnson for being a friend, following Jesus and writing a chapter about it; Carl Bunso for listening to the Spirit and making me laugh; Ryun Pavlicek for the many talks over coffee and all the encouragement along the way; Tom Nebel for being there 22 years ago in my time of need; Phil Phillips and Steve Smith for proof reading and being leaders who give me hope; David Johnson, Tom Fitzpatrick, Chris Steed, Reid Fitzpatrick and Ryun P. for seeking first His Kingdom and being willing to go against the flow as you lead; Dennis and Eve Fairchild for taking the step and being there from day one; and last but not least, Jason, Shante', George, Pete, Michael, Frank, Sandy, Fran, Anthony and all of those who are with me on the Journey. Without you there would be no story. It is truly a joy to serve along side of each and every one of you!

dEDICATION:

This book is dedicated to my family: Roxane, my wonderful wife and better half, who has been by my side for the last 22 years; Victor, Karis and Jonathan, who are my pride and joy. May you know and follow Jesus all your days.

Thank you for your love and patience along the way. I love all of you more than you will ever know.

tABLE *of* CONTENTS

INTRODUCTION
WHAT HAPPENED?

There was a time when the church was very powerful, in the time when the early Christians rejoiced at being deemed worthy to suffer for what they believed. In those days, the church was not merely a thermometer that recorded the ideas and principles of popular opinion; it was a thermostat that transformed the mores of society... Things are different now. So often the contemporary church is a weak, ineffectual voice with an uncertain sound. So often it is an arch defender of the status quo. Far from being disturbed by the presence of the church, the power structure of the average community is consoled by the church's silent and often even vocal sanction of things as they are. But the judgment of God is upon the church as never before. If today's church does not recapture the sacrificial spirit of the early church, it will lose its authenticity, forfeit the loyalty of millions, and be dismissed as an irrelevant social club with no meaning for the twentieth century. Every day I meet young people whose disappointment with the church has turned into outright disgust. Perhaps I have once again been too optimistic. Is organized religion too inextricably bound to the status quo to save our nation and the world? Perhaps I must turn my faith to the inner spiritual church, the church within the church, as the true ecclesia and the hope of the world.

---Martin Luther King, Jr.
penned in 1963 in his "Letter From A Birmingham Jail"

Has the church lost "its authenticity?" By its actions, has it "forfeited the loyalty of millions?" Is it currently being "dismissed" by many as an "irrelevant social club?" Have you recently met any young people whose "disappointment with the church has turned into outright disgust?"

Forty-eight years ago, Martin Luther King, Jr. warned his fellow clergymen that these things would happen if the church did not recapture the sacrificial spirit of the early church.

Hmm…maybe he was onto something.

Think about it. If you were to ask your friends to give you one word that best described the church in America, what kind of response do you think you would get? Do you think "sacrificial" would be at the top of their list? Would it be on their list at all?

Should it be?

What if you asked them to give you one word to describe Jesus? Do you think they would use the same adjectives that they used to describe the church?

Why do many people today describe the church with terms they would never use to describe Jesus Christ? Some of the words topping the list would be "judgmental," "money-hungry," "controlling," "self-centered" and "fake." I have actually heard each of these used by people to describe Christianity and or the church in America, but I have never heard anyone use such words when talking about Jesus.

Maybe it's just me, but I find this both confusing and disturbing. Christianity was founded on the life and teachings of Jesus. The Christian church is made up of those who claim to believe in Him and to follow His teaching. Then why is there such a disconnect between people's perception of Jesus and their perception of His followers?

Could it be that the church has become something other than what Jesus intended? Did He have in mind the construction of multimillion dollar buildings and pastors who achieve rock star status when He sacrificed everything and allowed Himself to be beaten and crucified? Is there any place in the Bible where Jesus encourages His followers to pursue their best life now? Should programs come before the basic needs of people? And is there any justification for the competition that we see among churches today?

The evidence is all around us. Steeple envy is everywhere.

Consumerism, competition and corporate America have infiltrated the church. They have left us with something radically different from what we read in the pages of the Bible.

However, there are people all over the world who are finding that there is more to Jesus and His Church than what meets the eye. Some like Martin Luther King, Jr. have found themselves turning to the church-within-the-church as the hope of the world.

I am one of those people, and maybe you are too. Or maybe you're a part of the ever-growing group who has all but given up on organized religion. I understand. After going to seminary and serving as a pastor for 13 years, I realized that I was in a similar place; as a result, I have spent the last four years rethinking much of what I was taught. This has led me on a fascinating journey of rediscovering Jesus and His Church.

If any of this resonates with you, I would encourage you to read on. I don't claim to have all the answers; nevertheless, I do believe that there are answers to be found. I also believe that there is a lot at stake. So whatever you do, don't give in and don't give up.

Don't give in to the status quo, and don't just continue going through the motions, particularly if you know that something isn't right. Also, don't give up on your search for truth. Even if you've been let down by those who should have brought you hope and encouragement, don't give up.

"Jesus said, 'Seek and you will find.'"[1]

I am one who continues to seek. In the process, I have discovered that although people, religion and church may fail you, Jesus never will. So I invite you to join me on this journey of rediscovery.

"Ask and it will be given to you; seek and you will find; knock and the door will be opened to you. For everyone who asks receives; he who seeks finds; and to him who knocks, the door will be opened" - Jesus (Matthew 7:7-8).

---

[1] Matthew 7:7

| CHAPTER ONE |

Holy Crap!

Have you ever watched the classic television series *The Twilight Zone*? Do you remember the eerie musical intro "Dee-dee-dee-dee, dee-dee-dee-dee...?" Can you recall the unforgettable voice of Rod Serling telling us, "You're traveling through another dimension...a journey into a wondrous land...whose boundaries are that of imagination... the sign post up ahead... your next stop—the twilight zone?"

Whether or not you're a fan of The Twilight Zone, most of us have at least seen an episode or two. Usually each one began with a scene that by all appearance is a snapshot out of everyday life. And then Mr. Serling entered to remind us that all is not as it appears. From there we were sucked into a story that usually went from normal to bizarre and sometimes even frightening, all the while enjoying the ride.

I will never forget being a kid and watching what has become my favorite episode of all time—"Eye of the Beholder." OH MY GOSH!! If you haven't seen it, do yourself a favor, and check it out. (It's on You Tube.) This particular episode involved a woman whose face had been horribly disfigured, so she had surgery to get it repaired. The storyline was absolutely genius and actually quite insightful.

As much as I enjoyed watching those shows, I must admit that I was always comforted by the thought that it was only television. Strange things like that don't happen in real life, only in TV shows and nightmares. It's all just a well-told story dreamed up from someone's imagination.

But what would happen if one day you woke up and found yourself in the middle of one of these bizarre tales?

C.R.A.P.

The year was 2007, and life was good. I had been married to the woman of my dreams for 16 years. We had just welcomed our third child into the world—little Jon, my "linebacker" as the delivery nurse called him. I was driving a pretty sweet ride, and we were living in our dream home. What more could a guy ask for?

I was also enjoying great success at work. My role had broadened, and the organization had grown exponentially in the six years since I had been there. We just moved into our new offices and were already talking about expansion.

I remember sitting in my new corner office one day, looking out at the beautiful landscaping and the giant palm trees (which we had shipped all the way from the west coast to Florida) and thinking to myself, "Life is good."

Now don't get me wrong. I wasn't knocking down crazy money like the CEO, but I also didn't have his responsibilities and stress. As it was, I had everything I needed and most things that I wanted. Shoot, I even got my first pin-striped custom suit, compliments of the company—you know, the kind with the personalized tag on the inside pocket of the coat that says "Exclusively Tailored for Vic Cuccia." By all accounts, I had made it.

However, things are not always as they seem. Sometimes what you see is not what you get, and it takes someone or something to help you see the forest for the trees. So when it comes to my story, this is the point where I could just imagine Rod Serling entering the picture. In that most memorable voice, he would begin his soliloquy with something like what he said in "The Shelter" episode: "What you're about to watch is a nightmare. It's not meant to be prophetic. It need not happen. It's the fervent and urgent prayer of all men of goodwill that it never shall happen, but in this place and this moment, it does happen...This is the Twilight Zone." [2]

So there I was, neither the richest nor the most powerful man on the block. But, I had all that I needed and much more than I ever

---

[2] "The Shelter." The Twilight Zone. Writ. Rod Serling. Dir. Lamont Johnson. Cayuga Productions. 29 Sept. 1961.

deserved. And then it happened. In what seemed like an instant, my world turned upside-down. It was as though I woke up one day, and everything was different. I began to see things through a different set of eyes, and I didn't like what I saw. In fact, some of it appalled me.

The things that once satisfied me now rendered little satisfaction. The "blessings" began to feel more like burdens. I felt as though I was dying on the inside. When I looked in the mirror, the man I saw was not the man I once knew. How could this have happened? I was doing all the right things, or so I thought.

You see, for the most part, I was a pretty good person. Most of my friends were good people as well, devoutly religious, conservative, right wing... Well you get the picture. And did I mention the fact that I was a...pastor? That's right. I was an associate pastor of a rapid-ly-growing evangelical church that was approaching "mega-church" status. What was supposed to be every minister's dream was slowly becoming my nightmare.

What went wrong?

I had gone to seminary and received my Masters of Divinity from a well-respected, evangelical school. (My degree, in itself, is quite humorous. After all, who can master divinity?) I was doing everything that was expected of me, and I was in a context where it was actually working. We had some 1,500 people in attendance on Sundays, and we had just finished a 12 million-dollar building project. How could something so right feel so wrong?

The way I would describe what happened is similar to that of the proverbial frog in the kettle. You've probably heard that if you put a frog in a pot of water that is room temperature and slowly turn up the heat, the frog will stay in it. He is unaware that the water is getting hotter and hotter—until eventually he becomes frog soup.

Well, the "pot" that I was in was the American church, and the water consisted of all the teachings, traditions and opinions of man that had crept in over time. The water was getting hotter and hotter, and I was dying from the inside-out without even realizing what was happening.

Then it hit me.

I had what I call my "Holy Crap!" moment.

The last ten years of my life felt like they were flashing before my eyes. I began to see how much I had changed, and not necessarily for the better. I went from being a guy whose heart broke for those considered outcasts and marginalized by society to being complacent within the confines of the church walls and rubbing shoulders with professional athletes and high-powered businessmen.

I know that there's nothing wrong with spending time with popular people; and there's something very alluring about being around those who are powerful in this world. And yes, I know that they need Jesus, too. The problem comes when we somehow find ourselves thinking that Jesus needs these people more than He needs the outcasts or those who have been marginalized. Of course, none of us would ever admit to believing such a thing. But if we were to judge what we truly believe by where we invest our time and resources, I think many of us might be surprised.

I can't help but be reminded of the time when Jesus was hanging out with a bunch of people who were disliked by the religious folks. The religious people did what they did best. They started talking behind His back, saying things like, "Why is He hanging out with all these sinners?" Jesus, never one to back down from a fight with the self-righteous, turned to them and said, "It is not the healthy who need a doctor, but the sick. But go and learn what this means: 'I desire mercy, not sacrifice.' For I have not come to call the righteous, but sinners" (Matthew 9:12-13).

So there I was, me, my pin-striped suit and a bunch of "righteous" people. This may be just fine for a lot of people, but for whatever reason, it was no longer fine for me. In fact, one of the reasons I call this my "Holy Crap!" moment is because basically, I felt like I was spending much of my time doing a lot of "holy C-R-A-P":

Coddling
Religious
Auspicious (and arrogant)
People

Call me naïve, but when I decided to give my life in service to God, I never envisioned many of the things that I found myself doing. Somehow I missed the passage of Scripture where Jesus said to go and put on a great show in My name, teaching those who serve to make perfect cappuccinos that you shall sell at the big event, along with well-packaged CD's of the messages that you speak out of My Word.

Regardless, we were some cappuccino-making, CD-selling, righteous folks. And man, could we put on a show! It was very well done and timed to the minute. Now I don't think there's anything wrong with doing things with excellence or having coffee at church services. Indeed, coffee is a necessity in many churches to keep the snoring and drooling down to a minimum. And when it comes to excellence, it might not hurt for someone to be honest with the lady who sings the solo so off-key that canines are covering their ears. But instead, we usually say something like, "Thank you, Sister. What a blessing."

So I get it.

I'm all for functioning with excellence and being relevant. But at what cost? And do we really need to have all the buying and selling going on? Marketing and fundraising seem to have taken the place of faith, prayer and following the way of Jesus. I remember being told, "If you ever plan on being a senior pastor, you will need to understand and accept that a big part of your job is being a fundraiser." In my kettle-warmed state, I often accepted this stuff at face value. After my "holy crap" moment, I began to look at these things differently, and at times literally say out loud,

"Holy crap!"

What has happened to the church?

Even worse, what has happened to me?

Scripture passages I had read started to come to mind, such as in Matthew's gospel when he wrote, "Jesus entered the temple area and drove out all who were buying and selling there. He overturned the tables of the money changers and the benches of those selling doves. 'It is written,' He said to them, 'My house will be called a house of prayer, but you are making it a den of robbers.'" [3]

Of course this passage couldn't possibly apply to what we commonly see in church today, could it? Here is what The Bible Knowledge Commentary has to say regarding this passage: "As Messiah Jesus entered the temple area, His indignation was directed toward those who had changed the character of the temple from a place of prayer into a place of corrupt commercialism. Many were making their living from the temple and the sacrifices purchased there." [4]

Could it be that Jesus had His own "holy crap" moment? Before you stop reading and label me an irreverent heretic, consider the situation. There was Jesus. He walked into church, and He literally flipped-out. He turned over tables and chased people out of the temple. John tells us that He had made a whip out of cords and drove them out. [5] I know this doesn't look much like the emaciated, blonde hair, blue-eyed American-made Jesus who we have come to know and love, but this is the Jesus of the Bible.

Why would He do such a thing? What if He were to walk into one of our church gatherings today? What would He do? Would He go and order a cappuccino before entering the bookstore to purchase a bracelet with His name on it, a CD series, and some "Testamints" to help with His coffee breath? Or would He maybe, just maybe, start flipping over tables and running people out? I don't know, but I think it's time that we're intellectually honest and at least start asking some of these questions.

Does the church in America today closely resemble what we see of the early Church in the Bible? Do those who lead the church live the same sacrificial lives we see portrayed by Jesus and His disciples? Is the church characterized by the same love that we see displayed from

[3] Matthew 21:12-13.
[4] John F. Walvoord, Roy B. Zuck, & Dallas Theological Seminary, *The Bible Knowledge Commentary: An Exposition of the Scriptures* (Wheaton: Victor Books, 1983), 68.
[5] John 2:15.

the One it claims to follow? And when people reject this American version of Christianity, what is it they're really rejecting?

These are just a few of the questions that had begun to plague me. So what do you do when you recognize there's a problem, and you're smack dab in the middle of it? I don't know about you, but if I'm in the pot, and I can feel the water beginning to boil, I'm jumping out faster than you can say, "Trinity Broadcasting Network."

And that's just what I did.

"The very credentials these people are waving around as something special, I'm tearing up and throwing out with the trash—along with everything else I used to take credit for. And why? Because of Christ. Yes, all the things I once thought were so important are gone from my life. Compared to the high privilege of knowing Christ Jesus as my Master, firsthand, everything I once thought I had going for me is insignificant—dog dung. I've dumped it all in the trash so that I could embrace Christ and be embraced by Him. I didn't want some petty, inferior brand of righteousness that comes from keeping a list of rules when I could get the robust kind that comes from trusting Christ—God's righteousness" (Philippians 3:7-9 *The Message Bible*).

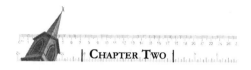

CHAPTER TWO

Isn't She Beautiful?

The church is a whore, but she is still my mother.
   ---St. Augustine

So I found myself wrestling with my own existence. There I was, a "man of God" (did you catch the tongue-in-cheek televangelist inflection there?), questioning my allegiance to the very institution that gives significance to so many—the church. Actually, it wasn't the historic Church that I questioned as much as the present-day state of the church in our country.

To me, the very thing that's supposed to be a channel of love, hope and redemption is becoming more and more self-indulgent. As a result, it's in danger of becoming functionally irrelevant. I'm sure there are many who disagree. I would argue, though, that a lot of churchgoers are so immersed in Christian subculture that they're out-of-touch with reality as well as with those who live outside of their myopic existence.

Actually, people are leaving (or staying away from) the church in huge numbers. And for the most part, Christians either act like they don't believe this is happening, or they don't care.

Now I know there are some religious people who, when they hear this perspective, stomp their feet in frustration and say, "This guy is crazy. The church is here to stay!"

Well, you know what? I actually agree. The Church is here to stay. I just wonder how much of the "church" we see in this country today is a good representation of Jesus and *His Church* as described in the Bible.

I think it's time to ask some hard questions. We need to make some realistic assessments and be willing to change, when change is necessary. I would also like to encourage those who have questioned their own sanity, morality or salvation as a result of wrestling with and/or disagreeing with the institutional church. You're not crazy, and you're definitely not alone.

People have ignored truth and reality for long enough. There comes a point when we have to quit acting like five-year olds with our fingers in our ears, making loud noises and yelling, "I'm not listening to you. You don't know what you're talking about. You don't exist. Blah, blah, blah."

The world around us does exist, and it has a voice. In fact, that voice should ring louder in our ears than the outspoken churchgoer who is determined to fight tooth-and-nail to have the drums turned down and the earrings removed from the song leader's ears.

It's time to look around, and it's time to listen. Most importantly, it's time to be honest. Let's stop avoiding the difficult and sometimes unvoiced questions and start willingly assessing the current state of the "church." In doing so, we might be able to better discern why local churches in America are experiencing this mass exodus.

You may have noticed that I've been using words like "us" and "we," which I assume is already making some religious folks uncomfortable. Fear not! I'm sure God allows consolation for those of us who think that other Christ followers won't make it to heaven because they say outrageous things or question the church. I mean, He has to. Right? He must make some kind of provision for all the denominations and sects who believe they're the "true church" that descended from the apostles. Maybe He'll give these people their own private rooms so they won't be so disappointed when others who are "less deserving" are allowed into heaven.

All that to say, feel free to ignore my assumptions that we're all on the same team. I just choose to believe that's how God sees it, so that's how I write.

Now, since that's out-of-the-way, let's get down to the *nitty-gritty*.

I know a lot of people who don't go to church. Many of them are good people; they just have no interest in organized religion, especially Christianity. While some polls have indicated that as many as 30% to 40% of Americans go to church each week, new studies are showing that percentage to be quite lower. The number of people who actually attend church on a regular basis in America is now believed to be less than 20%.[6] Something I have recently come to realize is that while a lot of people don't currently attend church, many of them did at some point in their lives.

I find that interesting. If I like something, I tend to go back to it. If I find a restaurant that's really good, it becomes a regular stop on the lunch rotation. If there's a band that I think rocks, then they'll be in the playlist of my iPod. If a book really impacts me, I'll probably read it again at some point.

Of course the opposite is true as well. For instance, when I recently saw a cashier chasing down a giant cockroach on the counter of a local fast-food restaurant, not only did I walk out before ordering, but I've never gone back since.

The church in America is in decline.[7] People who grew up in the church are leaving, and many who have never been simply have no interest.

So what's the problem?

What has made the church in our day so unattractive to so many?

---

[6] David T. Olson, *The American Church in Crisis* (Michigan: Zondervan, 2008), 29.

[7] The American church is in decline. This is a widely accepted and highly documented truth, although not that many people are talking about it. Probably the best and most current work on the subject is *The American Church in Crisis* by David T. Olson. In this book, Olson talks about the problem and documents the church's decline over the last 20 years. He also gives suggestions as to how to turn the tide. On page 183, he gives "Ten Necessary Changes for the American Church to Have a Bright Future". Number four states, "The best pattern for the mission of the American Church is the early church's attitude, model and mission strategy to the Greco-Roman world. (Olson, David T. in *The American Church in Crisis* (Michigan: Zondervan, 2008).)

BEAUTY

The Church you read about in the Bible was a beautiful thing. It was a place where love and hope could be found, a place where grace and acceptance was extended to all. People genuinely loved one another and took care of those who had need.

Socioeconomic status meant nothing, and people from all walks of life were accepted. The Church in the New Testament looked a lot like a reflection of the life that Jesus lived while He walked the earth.

Jesus' love was compelling, and He extended it to all people—prostitutes, drunkards, tax collectors, Jews, Gentiles and Samaritans. All were treated with dignity and loved by Jesus. He was totally comfortable going to places where religious people would never go, and He was always welcomed. Jesus had a way of being in the middle of it all without compromising who He was or feeling compelled to condemn those around Him.

So what happened to that Church?

Think about this: if you were to ask people who don't attend church what they think about Jesus and then ask them what they think of the church in America, would the response be the same? I would say that most people still have respect for Jesus while the church often falls into the category of irrelevant, judgmental or money-hungry.

So, we know from the statistics that churchgoers are bailing out. We also know that the un-churched aren't exactly lining up at the door either. The question is, "Why?"

Because in large part, the American church is gradually becoming less and less like Jesus. This isn't just my personal opinion, but it's also the opinion of countless individuals who have no desire to align themselves with evangelical Christianity today.

David Kinnaman and Gabe Lyons have done an excellent job uncovering this truth in their book *unChristian: What a New Generation Really Thinks about Christianity…and Why It Matters.*

Using the lens of the careful, scientific research we conducted, I invite you to see what Christianity looks like from the outside. In fact, the title of this book, unChristian, reflects outsider's most common reaction to the faith: they think Christians no longer represent what Jesus had in mind, that Christianity in our society is not what it was meant to be...They admit they have a hard time actually seeing Jesus because of all the negative baggage that now surrounds him. [8]

This is a far cry from what we see of the early Church that came on the scene shortly after Jesus' death. Read the following and think about whether or not this would characterize your personal church experience:

"They devoted themselves to the apostles' teaching and to the fellowship, to the breaking of bread and to prayer. Everyone was filled with awe, and many wonders and miraculous signs were done by the apostles. All the believers were together and had everything in common. Selling their possessions and goods, they gave to anyone as he had need. Every day they continued to meet together in the temple courts. They broke bread in their homes and ate together with glad and sincere hearts, praising God and enjoying the favor of all the people. And the Lord added to their number daily those who were being saved" (Acts 2:42-47).

Does the church look like this today?

How often have you experienced this kind of love and dedication among a community of people? What I find most intriguing in this passage is the fact that these early followers of Christ enjoyed "the favor of all the people." There was something compelling about this group. Apparently, this kind of commitment and devotion was attractive, even to those who were on the outside looking in.

The Message Bible puts that same passage in Acts this way: "People, in general, liked what they saw."

We get more insight as we read on...

"All the believers were one in heart and mind. No one claimed that any of his possessions was his own, but they shared everything they

---

[8]David Kinnaman, Gabe Lyons, *unchristian: What a New Generation Really Thinks about Christianity...and Why It Matters"* (Grand Rapids, Baker Books, 2007), 15.

had. With great power the apostles continued to testify to the resurrection of the Lord Jesus, and much grace was upon them all. There were no needy persons among them. For from time to time those who owned lands or houses sold them, brought the money from the sales and put it at the apostles' feet, and it was distributed to anyone as he had need" (Acts 4:32-35).

It's no wonder people liked what they saw! What an incredible display of love and compassion. Can you imagine being part of a community of people who cared for each other so much that they made sure there were no needy people among them?

The idea of sharing everything you have with others may seem a little overwhelming. Who really wants to sell their house, land and possessions to simply help others? Apparently a lot of people did! The key is that they actually wanted to help as opposed to being forced to do so. Out of their love for God and others, people sold land and houses "from time to time" to meet one another's needs. The Bible doesn't say that everyone did that or that they sold *everything* they had. It was simply a beautiful picture of true community—a place where people had a love for others that transcended the self-centered lifestyle that pervades our culture…and the church…today.

Just imagine,

"There were no needy persons among them."

As I wrestled with this reality, I found myself becoming less comfortable with many things I had been taking at face value. I just assumed that the way we had been "doing church" all these years was the way it was supposed to be done. After reading the New Testament with an open mind, and particularly the book of Acts, I began to question a lot of it. These were not just questions I could shrug off. They were questions that kept me up at night.

For instance, we read about the church sharing and sacrificing for one another in the book of Acts. How can we then turn our attention to the building of an institution that brings people together one or two days a week for this "thing" we call church? Today we *go* to church; back then they were *called* the Church. It wasn't something that you came to see and experience; it was who you were.

Often times today, the church is more focused on simply sustaining itself and its programs than it is on helping those in need. Salaries and building projects dominate the majority of the budget, while helping relieve the suffering of the needy has become an afterthought.

I'm not making a broad blanket statement about all local American churches. There are wonderful exceptions. Some churches truly get it and seek to mimic the compassion of Jesus and the early Church. Cornerstone Church where Francis Chan used to pastor is a great example. They give away 50% of everything that's given to them. What a beautiful representation of generosity!

But then there are churches—and lots of them—that don't even have a line item in their budget to help those in need. I have seen some churches that while they do have a benevolence budget, it's less than 10% of what's allocated for marketing. How bass-ackwards is that?

Maybe it's just me, but I would think that an organization whose Founder was basically born homeless, devoted to helping the needy, and loved the least of these, might want to make these things a priority. Jesus said that He came to preach good news to the poor and to free the oppressed. [9] Sadly, we're more concerned with our glossy invite cards than we are with helping the needy who are all around us.

I began to wonder what would happen if we just did the things that Jesus did and lived like the New Testament Church. Could we have lost this simplicity in the midst of all our planning, programming and methodology? Our institutionalized form of Christianity seems to have taken precedent over the simple methods found in Scripture.

Rather than just sharing truth and encouraging people to live it, we're hiring marketing consultants to help us brand and package the message in order to reach the masses.

But at what cost?

This isn't some *ShamWow* towel that we're selling, is it? And if we're going to be honest, we can admit that most of the people who we're trying to reach haven't shown much interest in our "product." Maybe that's because it's not a product to be marketed or a message to be

---

[9] Luke 4:17-19.

sold; maybe it's a life to be lived and shared in such a way that its message screams louder than any bumper sticker, billboard or bullhorn ever could.

So needless to say, when I heard there was a conference about the local church that was entitled "Isn't She Beautiful," not only did it catch my attention, but it actually made me laugh out loud. I thought, "Yeah, she's about as beautiful as the bearded woman at a circus side show." The last word that I would choose to describe the church as we know it today would be *beautiful*.

So what did I do? I went online to register, hoping to find a Cinderella out there among the many ugly step-sisters who we all know too well.

TRIP TO MARS

Before I knew it, I was on my way to somewhere I had never heard of in Michigan to learn about this *beautiful* thing called the *Church*. This was the same church that to me, seemed to be about as elusive as Big Foot and the Loch Ness Monster.

The conference was hosted by Mars Hill Bible Church where Rob Bell was the teaching pastor.[10] I had actually begun listening to their weekly podcast and found much of what I heard quite refreshing and challenging. However, nothing could have prepared me for what I was about to experience.

It all began when my buddy and I were on our way to the first session. We left the hotel on a cold Michigan morning in search of Mars Hill. We didn't put much thought into the drive to get there. After all, we had directions in hand, and we were going to a church that had

---

[10] Rob Bell is a polarizing figure in Christendom today. He has been labeled a heretic by some and is seen as a hero of the faith by others. Although I may not agree with all of his theology, I certainly acknowledge him as a brother in Christ and a man that God is using powerfully today. The reality is that God used him to speak into my life at a critical time, and for that I am very thankful. To those who are prone to use labels and cast stones, remember that evangelical Christianity has gained much of its heritage from the likes of Luther, Calvin and Wesley. I find it ironic that each of these men taught things that would not sit well with many evangelicals today; in fact, they would probably make most cringe. With that, let us always extend grace and mercy. And if we ever feel the need to rebuke and/or correct, may it all be done in the Spirit of Christ and for the cause of His Kingdom.

somewhere in the neighborhood of 8,000 members. How hard could it be? Even a directionally-challenged southerner in Michigan on a snowy day shouldn't have a problem with this one. Or so I thought.

Before long, we found ourselves approaching our destination and began checking out the address numbers. We carefully watched as the numbers went up, and then before we knew it, we had passed the place. How could you drive up and down a street three times and not locate the mega-church that's supposed to be right there? It was one of those times when you found yourself saying, "What the...?"

We continued to look and then said, "There has to be a sign somewhere. It's supposed to be right here!"

Finally, we pulled into the parking lot of an old mall that had a YMCA connected to it. As we triple-checked our directions and looked around, we finally realized that this old mall was Mars Hill Bible Church.

Didn't anyone tell these guys that if you want to have a BIG church, you need a BIG sign to go with your BIG shiny building? Apparently not. Not only was there literally no sign to be found, but when we went inside, we immediately realized that this was not your typical mega-church.

We walked into an old one-story mall that pretty much felt like we were walking into, um, an old one-story mall. The stores had been replaced with kid areas that were decorated and inviting but far from over-the-top. To my surprise, there was no bookstore where we could purchase all of Rob Bell's latest books, videos and sermon series. And nothing was more humorous than the look I got when I asked one of the volunteers where I could buy a cup of coffee.

I quickly realized that I wasn't in Kansas...er...Jacksonville anymore.

We then ventured into the auditorium. Once again, I was quite surprised by what I found. The set-up was simple with basic metal-framed plastic chairs. There was a relatively small stage, considering the room held somewhere around 3,000 people. The auditorium was uniquely set up "in the round," and there were four simple screens to display the words for the songs that would be sung. The conference would have no fog, moving lights or elaborate stage backdrop. We received some plain black-and-white printed materials containing the basic conference info that we needed to know. That was it. These people almost seemed as if they were unconcerned with slick marketing or impressing people with a shiny, decked-out building.

What I experienced at Mars Hill was the antithesis of what I had been living for the last seven years. It was like a breath of fresh air. I wondered how in the world a church could grow the way it had without using the normal techniques and tricks of the trade. (I mean church growth methods.) However, by the time the conference had ended, all of my questions had been answered by one simple act.

I will never forget when Rob spoke on the last evening of the conference. He's a hyper guy as it is, but this time he was about as giddy as a school boy seeing a naked lady for the first time. He told us how excited he was about this moment and how much he had looked forward to it all week. I assumed he was referring to the communion that we were about to share together. But I was utterly surprised when he talked instead about the conference and how many people were in attendance.

He told us that there were around 2,000 people there that week and that each of us had paid around $100 for the conference. Then he explained how much it actually cost them to put on the conference, which was somewhere in the neighborhood of $50,000 when all was said and done.

Then came the punch line. What made Rob so excited? What was he looking forward to all week?

I'll never forget what he said next. "That leaves us with $150,000, and I am so happy to tell you that we are giving it all away!"

He then gave us a detailed rundown of the organizations and the individuals whose lives would be impacted with the proceeds.

With that, the place erupted.

So what had drawn some 8,000 people to this church? It definitely wasn't billboards, signs or a nice building with cutting-edge technology. I suppose the persona of a dynamic teacher like Rob Bell could be the reason, but I didn't get the sense that any of this was about him. All I can say is that the place felt real. It didn't have that fake front that I had become so accustomed to knowing. People genuinely seemed to care, and everything was centered on the mission. It wasn't about a person or the show but about the mission of God and His love for broken, hurting people.

In reflecting on all this, I thought, "Man, that is beautiful."

Hmmm. Maybe there is a Cinderella out there after all!

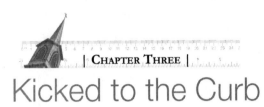

CHAPTER THREE

Kicked to the Curb

Christendom has done away with Christianity without being quite aware of it.
--- Soren Kierkegaard

Innocence is wonderful. As I watch my kids grow up, I'm amazed at how innocent they are. Granted, they're guilty in many ways and have confirmed their identity as "little sinners" time and time again.

But it's their innocence and naiveté that's fun to watch, like the time when one of our boys dropped trou in the backyard to take a poop like it was a part of everyday life. My wife Roxane ran outside, appalled, but too late to stop him. His response was, "The dog does it."

Or, like the way my nine-year old twins view members of the opposite sex—fun to play with, but they still have cooties. One night, Karis told Roxane how the thought of kissing anyone on the lips was yucky. However, as we all know, those thoughts and feelings change with time, opening up a whole other world of yuckyness that we're rarely prepared to face.

I'm not exactly sure at what point girls turned from *horrible* to *hot* for me, but it definitely happened.

I'll never forget my first girlfriend. I was in the fifth grade. She lived in my neighborhood, and we were in the same class. To this day, I don't know how it happened, but somehow I fell head-over-heels for her.

She made me feel like no one else on earth ever did. Of course at the time, I thought it was love. Now I realize it was probably just puberty. Regardless, I was infatuated with her. The first time we held hands, I thought my life was complete.

I just knew that I was going to get my first kiss soon, and I couldn't wait. But I would wait...and wait...and wait. And then the day finally came, not when I got my first kiss, but when she broke up with me. I got kicked to the curb, and I was devastated. She soon started hanging out with another kid, and I just couldn't believe that he was going to get that kiss instead of me.

So what do you do? I guess if you're mature, you pick yourself up and move on. If you're an immature, self-centered fifth grader like I was, you try to save face. How? You do everything you can to make her look stupid and to make yourself look good. And that's what I did. I said all kinds of horrible things about the girl who I once liked more than anyone else in the world. I was hurt, so I decided to deal with my pain by inflicting pain on someone else. I had to make her realize that she was wrong and that she must pay for her decision.

WALKING AWAY

I find it funny that people in church sometimes act like immature fifth graders. Hanging out together and enjoying each other's company is all good. But what happens if someone decides to leave? Do we handle the situation with love, grace and maturity? Or, do we sometimes look more like an immature kid who is set on defending his or her reputation?

While I was at the conference in Michigan, things had really come to a head. A friend called to inform me of some decisions that were announced during our weekly church staff meeting. Without divulging all the details, these were the kind of decisions that had been piling up on me. I disagreed with them but had no authoritative voice in the matters. In that moment, I knew the final straw had dropped, and like Joe Camel, my back was broken under the weight of it. That was when I decided to jump out of the pot that I call "American churchianity."

Graciously, God had orchestrated a series of events to really help me during this time. I was scheduled to interview Rob Bell for *HM (Hard Music)* magazine the day before all of this happened. Having been a concert promoter and the owner of an independent record label, I had some ties to the music industry. Somewhere I had heard that Rob was once in a punk band. Since I was already going to be there at this conference, I thought that it might be cool to interview him. I believed it would make a good story, how this guy who was once the front man in some punk band is now the pastor of one of the largest and most influential churches in America. So I made some calls, and we set it up.

On the day of the interview, I met my contact. She made some phone calls to try to locate Rob. The next thing I knew, she introduced me to Rob's brother, Jon Bell.

He was very apologetic. Apparently, Rob had been misinformed about the interview time and had already left the facility for the day. Jon apologized profusely, gave me his cell number and assured me that we would do the interview the next day. The delay wasn't a big deal; I figured that in the meantime, I would just continue to enjoy the conference.

The next day just "happened" to be the day that I received that call from back home. That was the day when my little world began to crumble around me. Questions flooded my mind as to what I would do, where I would go, and how I would take care of my family if I left the ministry. On that day, I also met Rob, and we did the interview. [11]

He was great, and when things wrapped up, we hung out for a few minutes and talked about music. I still remember how stoked he was when my buddy told him that the Police had just announced they were doing a reunion tour.

I then asked Rob if I could get a little feedback from him regarding the situation that I was facing. He said, "Sure," and so I fired away.

I'll never forget the conversation we had. I spilled my guts like road kill on a South Carolina highway to one of the few guys in the world who I thought might understand. I shared with him the things that I was wrestling with, things that I had seen and heard on the inside of what we call "the church," things that troubled me deeply. I confessed that I felt the need to resign from my position but feared what this would mean for me and my family.

---

[11] An unedited version of this interview can be found at www.steeple-envy.com.

How do you walk away from a generous salary when you have a wife and three kids, the youngest of who was only two months old at the time? I also feared the relational ramifications, having already learned that in our screwed-up little church world, leaving was sometimes like a divorce of sorts.

Some of you probably know what I mean. You decide to leave the church for whatever reason and the next thing you know, you're being treated like an infidel or someone who has just left the "family." Tony Soprano has nothing on some of these guys. Maybe you don't have to worry about anyone "offing" you or finding a horse head in your bed or anything like that. Instead, you're made to feel like you have just walked away from God. (And those who are close to God usually don't associate with those who walk away from God.) I'm not sure how we ever got to this place, but in the world of competitive church, this is not that uncommon.

I'll never forget the words that my new friend offered. "Man, I'm sorry. Trust me. I kind of know what you're feeling. But you don't need me to tell you what to do. You know what you need to do. What good is it if you gain the world but lose your soul? You're losing your soul. I can hear it in your voice and see it in your eyes. You would be better off walking away and going to paint houses or working at Starbucks, if that's what it takes for you to get back your soul. You know what you need to do. Just be sure that you and your wife are in total agreement, and everything will be OK."

He shared a few other words of wisdom in response to some questions I asked. Then he simply said, "How about I pray for you?"

I can't tell you how important that was to me. The advice was simple, but it was right on point. I needed someone to just look at me and call me out, and that's what Rob did.

It was true. I was dying on the inside. I had put on this plastic shell of a person to satisfy and please everyone who I thought needed satisfying and pleasing. But in the process, I lost much of my heart and soul. The fear of losing my job caused me to keep my mouth shut during times when I should have spoken up. Now it was a matter of conscience, and I found myself at a crossroads.

So he prayed for me, and I left with a resolve that I hadn't felt in a long time.

The defining moment came when I got home and talked to Roxane. She knew all about the struggles I had and shared many of them as well. We talked about everything that was going on and what we were feeling.

At one point, she just stopped and offered her perspective. She said, "Listen, when you were in seminary, we lived in a single-wide trailer, and we were fine." She gestured to our brand-new $350,000 house (or millstone, as I refer to it now) and continued, "We don't have to have all of this to be happy. As long as we have each other and Jesus, we'll be fine."

That was all I wanted to hear. I don't know how to explain it, but in that moment, I knew that everything was going to be alright. I hadn't given up on God—maybe the church (or the way that I had been defining it)—but not on Him. I knew that He would meet our needs just as He always had. I also knew that our needs may look a whole lot different than our wants, or current comforts for that matter. I was at peace with that. Maybe I was ready to just give it all up again to regain my soul. All I can say is that the weight of the world felt like it was lifted from my shoulders.

While this freedom felt great, I was also comforted by the thought that I could take a little time before making any move. This was a big decision with many questions to be answered. How do you gracefully walk away from a place and from people to whom you have given the last seven years of your life, many of whom you deeply love? How do you do that and honor God as well as everyone else in the process? And then when all is said and done, what do you do to make a living and take care of your family? The good thing was...I had time. I didn't have to make any rash decision. Maybe we could take a few months, save a little bit, and move back to South Carolina. Maybe there we could try to do this whole "church" thing differently—in a place where we had many friends, some who felt like family to us.

It has been said that the best laid plans of mice and men often go astray. Man, did they ever! Only days after returning from the conference, I found myself faced with a direct question. If answered truthfully, I would expose all that I had been feeling and what was going on in my heart. I had a decision to make. Do I do the Texas Two-Step and dance around the question to buy a little time, or do I just let it all out and be honest? What do you do when you know that honesty will cost you greatly? What if honesty could mean losing your job or losing your friends? Do you take the risk? Call me crazy, but that's what I chose to do.

That was on a Monday, and on Wednesday, I found myself meeting with the church "board." I thought that was kind of funny. I didn't really know we even had a church board until about two months earlier when my good friend and fellow staff member had resigned.

Based on godly wisdom and counsel, I ultimately decided that leaving quietly would be best. I turned in a detailed letter of resignation, and by Friday, I was cleaning out my office. Again, this was after being with this group of people for about seven years, six of those in a pastoral role.

There was no opportunity for goodbyes. It also didn't take long for the troops to be rallied and lines in the sand to be drawn. I tried to distance myself as much as possible, but there was no hiding the fact that I was portrayed in a less than favorable light at times. Even so, I had made the decision to allow God to be my defense, and so I willingly took a "few on the chin," so to speak. I don't know, maybe it was payback for what I had done to my childhood sweetheart many years ago. Regardless, it was definitely one of those "sucks-to-be-me-right-now" moments, that was for sure.

Now I'm not trying to make myself out to be the perfect saint here, and I'm no martyr. I'm sure that I didn't handle things perfectly, but I can sincerely say that I tried. I didn't have conversations with people about why I left, and I certainly didn't do anything to cause division or to disparage the church or any of the people involved. Nonetheless, my departure became an issue of "us" and "them." Before I knew it, many people were treating me like a modern-day leper put out of the camp for being unclean.

Those who I was very close to didn't want anything to do with me or my family. This includes many of whom I considered dear friends, some with which I spent countless hours helping their families in times of need. Although that was tough, this experience wasn't nearly as difficult for me as it was for my wife.

Those who know me can see that I'm a fairly even-keel guy. I don't get riled-up by too many things. But when I found myself holding my wife who was in tears because of the way her so-called friends were now treating her, I was ready to hit someone. I probably would have if it wasn't for the fact that in the midst of it all, my heart just broke; all I could think about was that *this was the church.* This is supposed to be the place where love and grace is reserved for even the worst of sinners, not a place where you shoot your own wounded just to save face or show your loyalty.

Think about this.

What if I had actually done something terribly wrong, divisive and downright evil? What should the response of Christians be in that situation? Shouldn't it be love and pity for the poor lost soul who has fallen away from God? Is there any Biblical precedent for the behavior that we often see in these situations? Whatever happened to the words of Jesus?

"You have heard that it was said, 'Love your neighbor and hate your enemy.' But I tell you: Love your enemies and pray for those who persecute you, that you may be sons of your Father in heaven. He causes His sun to rise on the evil and the good, and sends rain on the righteous and the unrighteous. If you love those who love you, what reward will you get? Are not even the tax collectors doing that? And if you greet only your brothers, what are you doing more than others? Do not even pagans do that? Be perfect, therefore, as your heavenly Father is perfect" (Matthew 5:43-48).

So ultimately, I thought trying to follow Jesus would probably be better than fighting against others who say they were also follow-ing Him. And I couldn't help but wonder how the rest of the world viewed all of this. What do people on the outside think when they see Christians acting this way? No wonder the American church is in decline. People don't care about the great show that we put on in Jesus' name if our relationships and lives simply duplicate those of the rest of the world—a world that we all know will chew you up and spit you out in a second.

When all was said and done, we ended up with a handful of friends. Maybe four or five families who showed they weren't as concerned about an organization or institution as they were about people.

I found this interesting and very encouraging. Honestly, some of these folks surprised me. God brought people who I would have never imagined to come alongside us with encouragement and comfort in our time of need. I was also reminded that throughout the Bible, God's love is displayed to people through people. He didn't use institutions to reach the masses. He used normal, everyday people for the most part. He used people whose hearts belonged to Him and whose greatest concern was expressing His love to others.

A NEW START

I have to admit that this small group of friends gave me hope again. I had hope that maybe there was a possibility that this thing called church could be done differently than what I had seen and experienced over the years.

About six weeks later, a good friend and I decided to invite some people over to cook-out, get to know one another better, and do a little Bible study.

I cannot tell you how refreshing this was. The pressure to be "on" was gone. We could just be ourselves and hang out.

Some interesting things started to happen, like when I received a phone call from Brent, a guy I had known from church. We weren't really close, but I got to know him when I spent some time with him and his wife during one of her surgeries. They were just good people, and we enjoyed one another's company. We discovered that we had some things in common, like during our days before following Jesus, we both used to burn the hippie lettuce and listen to bands like Pink

Floyd and the Doors.

Brent said to me on the phone, "Hey, I heard that you recently left the church. Do you mind me asking what you're doing these days?"

I hesitantly told him that a group of us were getting together to eat, look at the Bible, and try to figure out what the Church is really supposed to look like.

He went on to tell me that he and his wife actually left the church about six months before I did. He said they visited a few places, but they hadn't been going to church regularly because they just couldn't find anywhere that felt right. I don't know if they had given up on church, but he didn't sound as if they were actively looking either.

I'll never forget that conversation. The first thing I had to do was apologize. You see Brent left the church where I was pastoring—six months before I did, and I had no idea. In the midst of Sunday services and herds of people coming and going, I had no idea that this precious couple who had been at the church longer than me had disappeared six months earlier.

Brent's statement was one of those things that God used to confirm to me that something was wrong. How can someone who has been with a "church" for seven years leave without anyone really noticing, particularly when you consider how the early Church functioned? Those people broke bread together in each other's homes daily. They genuinely cared for and loved one another, helping those who had needs. To me, they sounded more like a family than a social club. Maybe the apostles themselves wouldn't have realized when a person left every time, but certainly someone would have.

I began to wonder what happened to *that* Church. Is it possible that the reason the church in America is in decline is because as each year passes, it looks less and less like Jesus and the Church we find in the Bible? Could it be that in the process of determining the "best practices" for church, we have abandoned the simple model prescribed in God's Word? Has that model been kicked to the curb in favor of a culturally-relevant experience, one that is aimed at satisfying the senses and providing everything that the typical American consumer wants and desires?

I had more questions than answers. But one thing I did know was that I was done trying to please consumer-driven church people. I didn't have any energy left to try to meet the needs of those looking for a great church. I simply wanted to know Jesus and be with people who were interested in trying to be the Church, whatever that looked like. I also began to wonder if such a thing as a great church even existed. To me, only one Church could really be found in Scripture, and that Church consisted of everyone who was following Jesus. Maybe it didn't matter where you met, whether it was a beautiful building, a coffee shop, a bar or someone's home. Maybe it wasn't about being better at all, just different.

I'll admit that questioning a 1,700-year old institution is a little scary. [12] In general, people don't dare question "the church," and pastors certainly don't break the unwritten code and ask questions that shouldn't be asked. But what if God never intended for the Church to be institutionalized? After all, Jesus and His early followers had no problem questioning and standing up to the religious leaders who had systematically removed God from their religious equation.

What if God is looking for people who are honest enough to call it like they see it? Could it be that this has less to do with rebellion and more to do with reform? Maybe those of us who resonate with these thoughts and feelings were created for such a time as this. Perhaps the

[12] You may wonder why I said that I questioned a "1700-year old institution," when in fact Jesus had walked the earth some 2,000 years ago. When Jesus ascended into heaven, the Church was birthed at Pentecost and looked nothing like an institution. The Church was more of an organic movement of people who were filled with the Spirit and led by the Spirit as they followed the way of Jesus. The Church was a movement that existed more in the margins of society than in the mainstream. Persecution and trials couldn't stop it because "it" wasn't something that was structured in such a way that it could be contained behind four walls. It was viral, so to speak, and it grew regardless of opposition. In 313 A.D., Constantine declared Christianity to be a legal religion and began compensating clergy and funding the building of churches directly from the Roman treasury. By 380 A.D. under the rule of Theodosius, Christianity was declared the official religion of the Empire. While many have seen this as a major victory for the Church, others believe that it actually may be the single most devastating thing to ever happen to Christianity. The Church changed from an organic movement to an institutionalized religion. Before long, Christianity began to look eerily similar to the same religion that Jesus opposed and that was ultimately responsible for His death. Although the Church has gone through much change and reformation over the years, for the most part, it remains institutionalized. It is this aspect of the church that I question.

undercurrent that's presently moving like a riptide through the waters of the church is something that God Himself has originated to bring a necessary change to the church as we know it.

Or maybe all of us who feel this way are just jaded, cynical, rebellious people who have been burned one too many times. All I know is that when I left a destructive life of drugs and alcohol, the only thing that made any sense to me and gave my life purpose was Jesus. In these moments, I found myself returning to this truth. And I wanted to know what He had to say about His Church.

As I found out years ago, who you are, where you've been, or what other people think about you isn't important. Jesus will never kick you to the curb—and that's good enough for me.

Chapter Four

Getting Naked

Na.ked:

Devoid of customary natural covering, bare; Being without addition, conceal-ment, disguise, or embellishment.

Since the Garden of Eden, nakedness has been quite taboo. Grant-ed, there are those who stray from the norm of society and do things that most of us would find uncomfortable and even strange.

For instance, the news did a report on a naked church. I don't know how many people saw it, but it ran on our local channel. According to the story, a group of people from a Virginia nudist colony have church services where, as they put it, "clothing is optional." Thankfully when they ran the piece, the camera angle was from behind the congrega-tion of about 10 people who were all seated. The pastor strategically stayed behind the pulpit.

When thinking of this church in terms of growth, it has little to no chance of making it. First of all, the guy leading was a bit rotund and quite hairy. Not that anything is wrong with that of course, but do you really want to see Santa Claus naked first thing in the morning? And this image doesn't include the rest of the congregation who were all at an age where gravity had already begun to take its toll. There would be a lot of distractions (no need for specifics), and wouldn't you always be thinking, "I wonder who sat here before me?" Let me move on before I digress.

Nakedness in general is uncomfortable for most, even when we move beyond the realm of the physical and talk more about the emotional and spiritual side of things. For the most part, people like to "clothe" themselves in such a way as to hide their deepest feelings, fears, thoughts and emotions. Very few of us are willing to bear our soul to one another and with good reason. We are most vulnerable in those moments, and many of us have been burned at one time or another by people we have let in and trusted.

MASKS

Church people are famous for covering what's really happening. We're experts at putting on masks to make everything look good. Somehow we've gotten to a place where people believe that if you struggle in any way, you must not be right with Jesus. If you don't have the Joel Osteen perma-smile on 24/7, something must be wrong. So we come in and out of church with our masks on, smiling and answering every question of "How are you?" with "I'm blessed. How are you?" You could have been arguing when you left the house, kicked the dog, and fought all the way to the church parking lot, but when you walk inside, it's time to put on the show.

This is one thing that has gotten harder and harder for me to do. I have begun to realize that part of my responsibility is to allow people to actually see that my life isn't perfect. Often people have this perception that pastors and those who are spiritually mature are the people who have it all together. Therefore, nobody wants to admit that they struggle and that everything isn't perfect all the time. So we put on our church smiles and act as though everything is great, even when it's not.

The movie Nacho Libre has a quite humorous picture of this outward show. Jack Black's character, Ignacio (Nacho), had been infatuated with wrestling ever since he was a young boy.

He then became a monk and worked in the same orphanage where he was raised. They had virtually no money for food, and as the cook, he was forced to serve nasty soup everyday to the orphans and other monks. This led to a scene where the following exchange took place while everyone was looking at these bowls containing this disgusting slop set before them:

Señor Ramon: What is this?
Ignacio: Leftovers. Enjoy.
Señor Ramon: There is no flavor. There are no spices. Where are the chips?
Ignacio: Somebody stole them.
Señor Ramon: Did you not tell them that they were the Lord's chips?
Ignacio: I was trying to!
Señor Ramon: You are useless, Ignacio!
Elderly Monk: Silence brothers! This is the worst lunch I ever had.
Señor Ramon: Your only job is to cook. Do you not realize I have had diarrhea since Easters?
Ignacio: OK. Maybe I am not meant for these duties. Cooking duty. Dead guy duty. Maybe it's time for me to get a better duty!

As a result, Ignacio decided to try his hand at wrestling, even though it was something forbidden among those who were "holy." So during the day, he was Ignacio the Monk with cooking duties at the orphanage, and at night, he was Nacho the Luchadore. He and his partner, Esqueleto, spent most of their time getting their butts kicked. Even so, they made money, which Ignacio used to buy better food for the orphans.

Then one day, Ignacio heard a squabble in the courtyard. He found Sister Encarnacion (who he liked and wanted to impress) breaking up a playful wrestling match between two of the orphans. At first he acted like it wasn't a big deal until the Sister reminded him that wrestling was ungodly. This caused Ignacio to put on his church mask, and we get the following exchange:

Nacho: Ok. Orphans! Listen to Ignacio. I know it is fun to wrestle. A nice pile drive to the face...or a punch to the face...but you cannot do it because it is in the Bible not to wrestle your neighbor.
Chancho: So you've never wrestled?
Nacho: Me? No. Come on. Don't be crazy. I know the wrestlers get all the fancy

ladies, and the clothes, and the fancy creams and lotions. But my life is good! Really good! I get to wake up every morning at 5 A.M. and make some soup! It's the best. I love it. I get to lay in a bed, all by myself, all of my life! That's fantastic!

Not only is this scene hilarious, but it's indicative of the way many Christians act. How many times have we all done something like this? We act as if life is great even though we may be deeply struggling.

I just love the line where he said, "It is in the Bible not to wrestle your neighbor." Not only was he covering up his hidden life of being a wrestler, but he resorted to making up a religious law to justify a stance that's not even supported by the Bible. People do this all the time, and the religious leaders were famous for it in Jesus' day.

Creating our own religious laws has left some of us with ridiculous rules and regulations which we attribute to being holy. Actually, they have little or nothing to do with what the Bible says. Fitting within this category is the old saying, "Don't drink. Don't dance. Don't chew, and don't go with girls that do" (or is that *guys?* Whatever…).

If you were to take some of what's taught today at face value, you would think there were Bible verses that commanded things like "thou shalt not dance;" "thou shalt not listen to rock music;" "thou shalt not drink alcohol;" "thou shalt not vote for this particular political party;" or maybe even "thou shalt not enjoy life!" And we wonder why people are not attracted to Jesus and His followers.

Then we have Ignacio's classic, sarcastic lines about how great and fantastic his pitiful life was. He was obviously miserable, but he could never come out and say it. Ignacio was a man of the cloth, so how could he admit that he actually despised much of what he did? His life was supposed to be great. At least that's what we were led to believe.

Well the reality is that sometimes life isn't great. In fact, there are times when life pretty much just sucks. Period. There, I said it. And you know what, lightning didn't strike and I was able to continue typing on my computer. Seriously, how can you read the Bible and not realize that life really sucked at times for people, even for some heroes of the faith?

Consider Joseph. He was sold into slavery by his brothers, falsely accused by some floozy, forgotten by those he helped and basically had a crappy go of things for about 13 years. Read the Psalms and listen to the heartfelt, unfiltered, and what many would consider irreverent cries of the psalmists. Everyone knows the story of Job. And have you ever read the litany of things that Paul went through? He was beaten with rods, whipped, starved, stoned (not in the Cheech and Chong sense, but pelted with rocks) and suffered in many other ways.

What all of these people realized and what we must realize is that God never promised us exemption from tough times. Jesus actually said we would face difficulties, but His promise was that He would never leave us or forsake us. So whether or not we're delivered from the trial, we can count on Him to be right there with us in the midst of the pain and struggle. Somehow we've come to the point where we think that if God was really there, we wouldn't experience the struggle at all. This is simply bad teaching and flies in the face of what Scripture tells us.

Consider the very words of Jesus:

"I have told you these things, so that in Me you may have peace. In this world you will have trouble. But take heart! I have overcome the world" (John 16:33).

Or how about these other verses:

"Consider it pure joy, my brothers, whenever you face trials of many kinds, because you know that the testing of your faith develops perseverance. Perseverance must finish its work so that you may be mature and complete, not lacking anything" (James 1:2-4).

"Dear friends, do not be surprised at the painful trial you are suffering, as though something strange were happening to you" (1 Peter 4:12).

"Be joyful in hope, patient in affliction, faithful in prayer" (Romans 12:12).

"And after you have suffered a little while, the God of all grace,

Who has called you to His eternal glory in Christ, will Himself restore, confirm, strengthen, and establish you" (1 Peter 5:10 ESV).

These are only a few examples that are found throughout the pages of Scripture. Pain and struggle are common place among God's people. Jesus is even referred to as a man of sorrows and a suffering servant. He struggled so intensely that He sweated blood. He endured more pain and suffering than we could ever imagine. If He is the One we follow, then why should we be surprised when we face difficulties in this life?

All of the early followers of Jesus experienced pain and persecution. Tradition tells us that each of the apostles suffered, and ten of the original 11 (Judas excluded) were killed as a result of their faith in Jesus.

I think we can gain a lot of insight from Paul when we consider the great sufferings he endured as a result of following Jesus. Look at what he said about facing difficulties and wearing masks:

"Since God has so generously let us in on what He is doing, we're not about to throw up our hands and walk off the job just because we run into occasional hard times. We refuse to wear masks and play games. We don't maneuver and manipulate behind the scenes. And we don't twist God's Word to suit ourselves. Rather, we keep everything we do and say out in the open, the whole truth on display, so that those who want to can see and judge for themselves in the presence of God" (2 Corinthians 4:1-2 The Message Bible).

Paul thought it such a privilege to be part of what God was doing that he wasn't willing to allow a little persecution and hard times to discourage him. He also wasn't interested in playing games and putting on a mask. Paul was wide-open, so to speak, and you could "read him like a book." He didn't twist God's Word for personal gain or to make himself look good, and he didn't appear too worried about what other people thought. The most important thing to Paul was being real and honoring God with his life.

I think we all have something to learn from the Apostle Paul. What matters most is what God thinks, not the opinion of those around us. We should be less concerned with impressing people with our dressed-up religious lives and more concerned with being authentic and joining God in what He's doing in the world today.

AUTHENTIC LIVES

If there is one thing that's missing in the church in America, it's authenticity. People are longing for real relationships with others, and ultimately with God, whether or not they realize it. The problem is that authentic expressions of community and faith have become more difficult to find. In fact, many have quit looking to the church, and instead, cite it as cold, judgmental, fake and the list goes on.

As I was typing this, I heard an email come in and decided to check it. Someone had sent a comment on one of my recent blog posts. I kid you not; this was what I read:

Your message was so true. I have been hurt by church family, and it is not pretty. The sad thing is, some don't realize how much they are hurting people. I haven't been to church since I moved on the south side 6 years ago. I have church at home by watching it on T.V. I miss the fellowship. God has been good to me, and I will never stop loving Him because of what people do.

I was a Sunday school teacher of ages 5-11, and I was also over the youth outreach group. I loved all the kids so much, and it hurt me to leave that church. I couldn't take how they were treating people, especially young people who were coming.

I don't like hypocrites. God sees us all the same. Ever since leaving there, I feel like I really see the love of God and how He really is. He loves us all. Just one example: This teen started coming to our church, and he had long hair. At an outing one Saturday, I heard a couple of older men tell him he needs to get his hair cut if he was going to come to the fellowship outings. That young man never came back, and he was so upset. I am sorry, but that is not love. That is control. I say get the people saved, and if God feels they need to change something, let Him deal with his heart. Some things are better left to God. Ok. I am done but just wanted to say thanks. I was looking for a church to visit, and your church jumped out at me. So I am sure I will be visiting soon. Thanks for that message. God bless.

This is not an uncommon story. Out there are thousands of men and women who have had similar experiences, and as a result, have left the church. Their faith may be intact, but they find themselves trying to live the Christian life on their own. And what about the countless people who have had experiences like the young man described in her email comment? Should we fault them for their negative or even hostile thoughts about God and His Church?

Consider this recent blog that I posted titled "I don't really like church":

A phrase that I often hear these days is "I don't really like church." That may not be an exact quote, but I hear that communicated in different ways quite a bit. In fact, rumor has it that a pastor even said that from the stage this past Sunday.

Church has fallen out of favor with many today. Right now I am sitting in Panera Bread, and there is a guy sitting next to me, and I am going to turn to him right now and ask him what he thinks about church, and then I will write his response. Seriously, I am going to do this. Hold on.

OK, I did it, really I did. I found out the guy's name was Ron, and the conversation went something like this...

Me: Hey, I'm sorry to bother you, but can I ask you a question?

Ron: Sure.

Me: What do you think about church?

Ron: In what context?

Me: I don't know. I was just wondering what you thought about church. Do you go to church? What's your opinion of church in general?

Ron: Well, I became a Christian in 1986. At first when it was just me, Jesus and my Bible, everything was great. Then I started going to church, and it was OK for a while, I guess. Then after a while, I started to see a lot of stuff, and well, I don't know. I know it is bad to say this, but it got political, or maybe it was just people's egos that got in the way. The church ended up going through a split and some other stuff. So eventually I just stopped going.

Me: That's hard.

Ron: Yeah, it seemed like people had more bad things to say than good. For instance, in my denomination, people would really slam Catholics, and I pretty much just listened and went along with it. Not too long ago, a friend of mine was in a situation where he was really in need. The Catholics were the ones who helped him out. No questions asked. They just helped him in his time of need. They helped him when people from my denomination wouldn't lift a finger. If I were to talk to someone from that group now, I would be cordial. But I can tell you, if they ever said anything bad about the Catholics, I would tell them to take a hike! So when it comes to church, I guess I can take it or leave it to tell you the truth.

Me: Man, I'm sorry. It sounds like you have seen some ugly stuff along the way...

There was more to our conversation, but I think you get the gist. Ron didn't come out and specifically say, "I don't like church," but he clearly isn't a big fan.

Our conversation was a good one, and as it continued, he reminisced about his time leading a small group for singles in the church he attended. He told me a few stories, like the time after one of their meetings, they all decided on a whim to just go swimming with all their clothes on. Then there was the time that they ended up helping a homeless guy. He had a smile on his face, and you could tell it really meant something to him. He said that he misses that at times.

This makes sense to me because those are the things I love about "church," not necessarily swimming with my clothes on, but being with people, doing life together and serving God. And the reality is that the things that turned Ron off, turn me off as well. In fact, when he was finished, he asked me what I thought about church. So I told him that as far as I could tell from reading the Bible, church is all about people. It was never described as a place or something we do; it is the people who gather. I went on to say that there are a lot of things about church that I don't like and that I wondered if God liked them either.

Can you believe it? What are the odds that I would get that kind of response from the first guy I asked? Unfortunately, pretty good these days. When the church becomes an institution or an organization rather than the life-giving organism described in the Bible, I think we're in trouble. But that's where we find ourselves today. Many people see "church" as somewhere they go or this entity that has a life of its own. Nothing could be further from the truth. We are the Church, and the Church has life because we have life. The Church reaches out to those in need when we reach out to them. The Church also can be inward and self-absorbed if we become inward-focused, self-absorbed people.

While the church may not be at the top of the opinion polls today, Jesus is still held in high regard. His love is still compelling, and His Spirit is still at work in people's lives. Just during a short conversation with Ron that day, I saw a part of him come alive as he recounted the times that he was "being the Church" with others.

So what's it going to take for him and others like him to re-engage or engage for the first time? As simple as it sounds, I think that they need to meet Jesus. They need to meet the Jesus that is alive and well, living in His people, and they need to see the beauty of the Church lived out before them. There are too many cheap substitutes these days. People are looking for the real thing.

Personally, I think it's time we owned some of this. I also think it's time to ask some of the hard questions and talk about things that have been left unsaid for too long. As a pastor, I have been troubled by those times when I found myself in agreement with jaded Christians, people from other religions, agnostics and even atheists regarding their opinions of "Christians" and the church in America. However, the more stories I'm told, like the one in the email commenting on my blog and like the one from my conversation with Ron, the more I understand why.

So rather than ignore many of the issues and questions that have plagued me over the last few years, I have decided to at least talk about them. Frankly, I'm tired of playing religious games and wearing masks. Life is too short. I can no longer allow myself to be more concerned about not rocking the boat of the religious right than genuinely seeking and speaking truth. Jesus spoke truth and asked hard questions with little regard to what it would cost Him. As His followers, I believe we are obligated to do the same.

For me, this is an exercise in honesty. I have decided to be as open as possible regarding my life as a pastor and what I have seen and experienced along the way. As I continue to bear my soul on the following pages, I want to make it clear that I sincerely love God, and I love His Church. My intention is not to point the finger and walk away. My hope is that what you read will begin a conversation that in turn may be used to bring about some much-needed change.

That being said, I feel very little obligation to protect religious systems or institutions. There has been a lot of hiding behind positions and traditions within the church. I believe that out of fear, we have allowed many things to go unchecked for too long. So if at times my words seem harsh, insensitive or sarcastic, it's probably because that's their intention. My hope is that as you laugh, and at times are even disturbed by what you read, you will be compelled to take some sort of action.

The dichotomy of how people view Jesus and how they view His followers and the church is tragic. For the most part, people find Jesus and His teachings compelling and attractive while the church is seen in a less than favorable light. I have to believe that this breaks God's heart, and therefore, it should break ours as well.

The way I see it, we have some decisions to make. Some people will choose to give up and leave the church, like the girl who sent me the email and like so many others have done. Then there are those who will give in and tow the party line and pretend like everything is OK, even though they know it's really not. Lastly, there is a small group of people who will choose to be agents of change in this time of great need.

What about you? Are you one of those people who is tired of it all and about to quit? Are you content with just going through the motions and acting like everything is OK, although there are things that bother you deeply? Or are you willing to be honest and be used by God to help strip away some of the things that have made the church undesirable to so many?

To be completely honest, I don't know if the institutionalized church will ever change enough in our lifetime to "enjoy the favor of the people" as the early followers of Jesus did. However, that doesn't mean we should give up. The good news is that the Church is not an institution. The Church, as described in the Bible, consists of those who love and follow Jesus. So in that sense, there is and always will be hope.

We have the ability to bring about change simply by the way we live. The following exchange between Jesus and one of the religious leaders of His day says it all:

"Teacher, which is the greatest commandment in the Law? Jesus replied, 'Love the Lord your God with all your heart and with all your soul and with all your mind. This is the first and greatest commandment. And the second is like it: Love your neighbor as yourself. All the Law and the Prophets hang on these two commandments'" (Matthew 22:36-40).

Could the future of the church hang on these two commandments as well? Can we really strip it down to something so simple, and can a handful of people really make a difference? We would do well to remember that it was Jesus, the One we follow, Who made such a statement.

He chose 12 ordinary men who would ultimately be used to change the world.

CHAPTER FIVE

Losing My Religion

That's me in the corner. That's me in the spotlight. I'm losing my religion, trying to keep up with you, and I don't know if I can do it...
--- R.E.M. from the song "Losing My Religion"

Recently I went to lunch with a guy who told me that he pretty much had me figured out. He said something like, "You really messed me up this past Sunday. Just when I thought I had you figured out, you come from a different angle. I can usually count on you for a heavy dose of 'religion is bad; Jesus is good,' and this weekend you didn't go there. Man, you messed me up." We both laughed as we ate our tabouli or whatever we were eating that day.

The fact is, it was funny but pretty much true. I used to like religion. In fact I was actually quite religious for a time. (Sorry to anyone who knew me then. I mean that.) If you would have asked me, I would have said that I wasn't religious, but I was.

I know a lot of religious people. Most of them are no fun to be around, and some of them are just plain weird. When I read the Bible, Jesus doesn't seem weird to me. He actually seems like a pretty cool guy, the kind of guy you'd like to hang out with and be like. He talked in everyday language and didn't hesitate to stand up to religious people who thought they were better than everyone else. He did things that religious people didn't like and said things that ticked them off. He was a rebel of sorts. Maybe that's why I like Him. It's also why they planned and plotted to kill Him.

Have you ever thought about the fact that Jesus was brutally beaten and ultimately killed by devoutly religious people? If you haven't read the Bible, I encourage you to check this out for yourself. The most religious people of that day, specifically the religious leaders, were the ones who killed Jesus. Why would those who were supposed to be following and serving God do such a thing? Had their religion become so important to them that they lost sight of God?

If the religious leaders of that time could be so deceived as to lose sight of God and not recognize Him when He showed up in their midst, isn't it possible that the same thing could happen today? I'm not saying this is absolutely the case; I'm just asking whether or not it could be possible. By the way, have you ever seen some of the preachers on TV? OK, enough said.

JESUS VS. RELIGION

So, if many of the religious leaders of Jesus' day totally missed it, and if there is at least a chance that religious leaders today could totally miss it, wouldn't we do well to ask some questions? Questions can often help us discern whether or not we're on the right track. Questions also keep people honest.

But how did we ever get to the place where asking questions about the church or its leaders is considered irreverent or wrong? This is crazy to me, particularly when you consider that Jesus did a lot of questioning when He walked the earth. He openly questioned the religious leaders regarding their practices and their motives. And He had no problem pointing out that their motives were wrong and even evil at times.

Matthew's gospel has a section where we see that Jesus went on a rant of sorts against the Pharisees. He rebuked them publicly and pulled no punches in the way He described their hypocrisy. This passage of Scripture has become known as Jesus' Seven Woes to the Pharisees. I have included a portion of it below. I would encourage you to read the following passages and then make your own determination as to what Jesus thought of the religious leaders of His time.

"Woe to you, *teachers of the law* and *Pharisees* (religious leaders), you *hypocrites!* You shut the kingdom of heaven in men's faces. You yourselves do not enter, nor will you let those enter who are trying to. Woe to you, *teachers of the law* and *Pharisees, you hypocrites!* You travel over land and sea to win a single convert, and when he becomes one, *you make him twice as much a son of hell as you are*" (Matthew 23:13-15).

"Woe to you, *teachers of the law* and *Pharisees, you hypocrites!* You give a tenth of your spices—mint, dill and cummin. But you have neglected the more important matters of the law—justice, mercy and faithfulness. You should have practiced the latter, without neglecting the former. *You blind guides! You strain out a gnat but swallow a camel.*

Woe to you, *teachers of the law* and *Pharisees,* you *hypocrites!* You clean the outside of the cup and dish, but inside they are full of greed and self-indulgence. Blind Pharisee! First clean the inside of the cup and dish, and then the outside also will be clean. Woe to you, teachers of the law and Pharisees, you hypocrites! You are like whitewashed tombs, which look beautiful on the outside but on the inside are full of dead men's bones and everything unclean. In the same way, on the outside *you appear to people as righteous but on the inside you are full of hypocrisy and wickedness*" (Matthew 23:23-28).

Are you surprised at all by the tone that Jesus used when He addressed the religious leaders? If you were to visualize the scene, what mental picture comes to mind regarding His demeanor? Go back and look at how He describes these people. What specific things does He point out?

So how do *you* think Jesus viewed the religious leaders of His day?

In all fairness, we probably shouldn't judge Jesus' attitude toward this group of people solely on what we see in one chapter of the Bible. So let's take a look at a few other things Jesus said about them. These next few passages give us some insight as to how Jesus spoke to His disciples about the Pharisees.

"Jesus called the crowd to Him and said, 'Listen and understand.

What goes into a man's mouth does not make him unclean, but what comes out of his mouth, that is what makes him unclean.' Then the disciples came to Him and asked, 'Do you know that the *Pharisees* were offended when they heard this?' He replied, 'Every plant that My heavenly Father has not planted will be pulled up by the roots. *Leave them; they are blind guides.* If a blind man leads a blind man, both will fall into a pit'" (Matthew 15:10-14).

"When they went across the lake, the disciples forgot to take bread. 'Be careful,' Jesus said to them. 'Be on your guard against the yeast of the Pharisees and Sadducees.'

"They discussed this among themselves and said, 'It is because we didn't bring any bread.' Aware of their discussion, Jesus asked, 'You of little faith, why are you talking among yourselves about having no bread? Do you still not understand? Don't you remember the five loaves for the five thousand, and how many basketfuls you gathered? Or the seven loaves for the four thousand, and how many basketfuls you gathered? How is it you don't understand that I was not talking to you about bread? *But be on your guard against the yeast of the Pharisees and Sadducees.' Then they understood that He was not telling them to guard against the yeast used in bread, but against the teaching of the Pharisees and Sadducees*" (Matthew 16:5-12).

"Then Jesus said to the crowds and to His disciples, 'The *teachers of the law* and the *Pharisees* sit in Moses' seat. So you must obey them and do everything they tell you. *But do not do what they do, for they do not practice what they preach.* They tie up heavy loads and put them on men's shoulders, but they themselves are not willing to lift a finger to move them. *Everything they do is done for men to see.* They make their phylacteries wide and the tassels on their garments long; they love the place of honor at banquets and the most important seats in the synagogues; they love to be greeted in the marketplaces and to have men call them Rabbi'" (Matthew 23:1-7).

Think about it.

Jesus was training the group of men who would carry His message on to the world after He left. Isn't it interesting that He specifically warned them to be sure that they don't follow in the footsteps of the religious leaders of their time? As if that wasn't enough, consider the following exchanges between Jesus and the religious leaders:

"So the *Pharisees* and *teachers of the law* asked Jesus, 'Why don't your disciples live according to the tradition of the elders instead of eating their food with unclean hands?' He replied, 'Isaiah was right when he prophesied about you hypocrites; as it is written: *"These people honor Me with their lips, but their hearts are far from Me. They worship Me in vain; their teachings are but rules taught by men. You have let go of the commands of God and are holding onto the traditions of men." And He said to them, 'You have a fine way of setting aside the commands of God in order to observe your own traditions!"* (Mark 7:5-9).

"'No servant can serve two masters. Either he will hate the one and love the other, or he will be devoted to the one and despise the other. You cannot serve both God and money.' *The Pharisees, who loved money,* heard all this and were sneering at Jesus. He said to them, '*You are the ones who justify yourselves in the eyes of men, but God knows your hearts.* What is highly valued among men is detestable in God's sight'" (Luke 16:13-15).

(Speaking to the Pharisees), "*You snakes! You brood of vipers! How will you escape being condemned to hell?*"(Matthew 23:33).

As you can see, Jesus used strong words when discussing and addressing the religious leaders during that time. He had no problem pointing out the differences between their priorities and God's priorities and that their hearts were not in line with God's heart. They had the appearance of something good, clean and righteous, but Jesus called them evil. They allowed their own traditions to replace what God had called and appointed them to do. Somehow they had gotten so far off track that they actually missed God when He showed up.

MODERN DAY PHARISEES?

I wonder how Jesus would fit in the box of American Christianity? What would He say to the religious leaders in our country? How would He react if He showed up to "church?" Would He be in awe of the amazing buildings that we have built in His name? Would He attend a church that is multi-site, and if so, would He go to the main campus or a satellite show? What would He say to the pastor that's rolling phat in his Bentley? Would He appreciate the luxury of the ministry's private jet so that He could be comfortable as He travels to His next stop?

How about if Jesus popped in on the church budget meeting? Would He be pleased with the way finances are allocated? I wonder if He would be as impressed with those who dress in their "Sunday best" as they are with themselves? Would He like the way we do our capital campaigns, or would He maybe have some suggestions for us? How do you think He would view the overall system?

As a follower of Jesus and a leader in *His Church*, those thoughts put the fear of God in me. Maybe I'm just over-thinking the whole thing. Or maybe we're in danger of turning something beautiful into a system made up of our own practices and traditions. Could we have created a religious system like that of the Pharisees which required very little of God's presence or intervention to succeed? Could our definition of success be flawed in the first place?

The reality is that you can grow a *church* in America with little to no help from God. People do it all the time. There are techniques and methods that can be used to attract people to a certain place at a certain time. And if you're not that creative, you can always hire consultants to help you. I have literally sat in meetings with marketing consultants who were paid to come and help market the church. This is not much different than the business world. You pay them a pretty penny, and they help you brainstorm as to how you can best sell your product.

I know this sounds crazy, but it's true. They'll tell you what series you should preach at a particular time of the year in order to draw the biggest crowd. Then they'll let you know what words you should and shouldn't use in the titles in order to attract certain people. They'll design eye-catching series logos to help you sell CD's and create glossy invite cards. They'll even coach you through your radio spots if you desire.

So if you want to grow, there are many ways to do that.

But does growth always equal success?

What does success look like in God's Kingdom? Does it mean more people and bigger buildings? Or does it simply look like the changed life of an individual whose heart now belongs to God? Nowhere in the life of Jesus do we see "success" the way we often define it today. He wasn't rich. He didn't own a lot of stuff, and He didn't seem that concerned with whether or not He had a big crowd. In fact, He seemed to purposely thin out the crowd at times by the things He said. And as we have seen, He certainly wasn't respected by other religious leaders. So was He successful or not?

Jesus didn't come to propagate a religious system. What's more, He often violated the very system that was in place at the time. Although He stood against the system, He always did the will of the Father. The system had become corrupt; for that reason, God stepped into the middle of it, bringing grace, truth and love, embodied in Jesus Christ.

I would say that Jesus successfully demonstrated the heart of God to a world that was being driven further and further away from God by religion. The religious system had become a barrier between God and everyday people. Rather than being an invitation into a relationship with God, the system was set up in such a way that it created what seemed like insurmountable barriers to those on the outside. In essence, Jesus shatters those barriers and says, "Everyone is invited in."

Maybe the heart and love of Jesus is what's missing from many churches today, the heart that says, "God loves you and wants to have a relationship with you...regardless of who you are or what you have done." Jesus displayed this kind of love throughout His life. There probably isn't a better example than when He encountered a woman caught in the act of adultery.

"The teachers of the law and the Pharisees brought in a woman caught in adultery. They made her stand before the group and said to Jesus, 'Teacher, this woman was caught in the act of adultery. In the Law, Moses commanded us to stone such women. Now what do You say?' They were using this question as a trap in order to have a basis for accusing Him.

"But Jesus bent down and started to write on the ground with His finger. When they kept on questioning Him, He straightened up and said to them, 'Let any one of you who is without sin be the first to throw a stone at her.' Again He stooped down and wrote on the ground. At this, those who heard began to go away one at a time, the older ones first, until only Jesus was left, with the woman still standing there. Jesus straightened up and asked her, 'Woman, where are they? Has no one condemned you?' 'No one, Sir,' she said. 'Then neither do I condemn you,' Jesus declared. 'Go now and leave your life of sin'" (John 8:3-11).

This is a beautiful picture of God's love for all people. Here you have a woman who Scripture says was caught in the act of adultery. Regardless of one's morals, most people would agree that adultery is wrong. Not only is it a violation of God's law, but most would say that living like this is destructive and hurtful to others.

Religion is personified in this story by the Pharisees and teachers of the law. As we see, religion condemns both the actions and the individual as well. God, on the other hand, is personified by Jesus. He does not condemn but rather comes alongside the individual, even defending her. Only after He showed her love by standing next to her in the face of her accusers, did Jesus say, "Go and leave your life of sin."

So reflecting on this story found in the Bible, I feel compelled to ask the question, "Who does the church of our day resemble more? Does it today look more like the Pharisees and teachers of the law, with rocks in hand standing ready to condemn the filthy sinner? Or does it look more like Jesus who comes alongside and stands next to the one living a sinful, destructive lifestyle, letting them know that they are loved by God?

BODY PIERCING IN THE SANCTUARY

I never could have imagined the firestorm of emotions and religious backlash that we would experience as a result of simply trying to be Jesus to a group of kids in the small town of Lexington, South Carolina. Admittedly, I was young and somewhat naive, not realizing that the "Bible Belt" could be a place of comfort for some, while at the same time whip the rear-end of others.

Our goal was to reach out to kids, many of whom would normally never walk into the doors of a church. We would provide a cool place for them, quality live music, and a staff of people who loved God and wanted to show that love to anyone who walked through the doors. The plan was to provide a safe place for kids to go on the weekends and to share the love of Jesus with them. At the time, the idea seemed good, and everyone was excited about it. Until it actually worked!

For our first event, we brought in the bands MxPx and Rocketboy. I don't think anyone expected a punk rock show in Lexington to draw that many kids, but it did. More than 300 people showed up that night, from jocks and cheerleaders to punk rockers with multi-colored hair, liberty spikes and multiple piercings. They were all together in one room, enjoying a good time in a positive, safe environment that was staffed with people from our church.

The event was awesome, and for the most part, everything went fairly well. Of course you can never be prepared for some things, like when part of the sound system caught on fire during the first band's performance.

And then there was the kid who decided to try and pierce his eyebrow with a safety pin. The operative word here was "try." One of our volunteers noticed a group of kids gathered in a circle, so he began to walk over to them. He arrived just in time to see this kid in the middle look up, which caused the whole group of them to fall out in laughter. He had successfully stuck a safety pin under his eyebrow. But what he didn't realize was that it had come out about an inch above his eyebrow. So when he clipped it together and looked up, his eye was actually held wide-open by the safety pin, so he couldn't even blink! Extremely stupid, but actually pretty funny.

We learned a lot and saw things we could certainly improve, such as security. Nonetheless, when all was said and done, everyone involved deemed the night a huge success. We had hundreds of kids come out, many of whom were unchurched. All of them not only heard about the love of Jesus, but they saw it in action. Our volunteers served and showed God's love to those kids regardless of how they looked or acted.

Word about the night swept through our little church and the monster of religion didn't take long to rear its ugly head. While most were supportive, there were those who protested based on what they had heard. One of the biggest concerns was that we were being "too worldly" by allowing that kind of music and those kinds of people to come into "our church." Of course, the whole premise here was that the *church was ours* and was more about the place where we met and less about the people who gathered there. Regardless of how flawed their point of view was, they didn't like it.

This matter all came to a head when a meeting was called with some of the church leaders and those most vocally opposed to this ministry. I will never forget sitting in that meeting with a good friend who had been instrumental in helping me put the concert together. We watched as emotions ran high and listened to how we were responsible for compromising and conforming to the world.

There were a lot of things said during that meeting. The most outrageous came from someone who gave his commentary on "those people," referring to some of the guys in the band. He proceeded to declare, "There is no way you can convince me that the Holy Spirit lives inside someone like that."

His proclamation prompted the question, "What do you mean when you say, 'someone like that?'"

He fumed and responded, "Someone covered with tattoos and having their body pierced like that!"

In the name of religion, this gentleman had taken it upon himself to decide who God could forgive, love and use, based solely on their outward appearance. This broke my heart and was the first of many times that I have seen the ugliness of religion up-close-and-personal. To think that this guy could be so judgmental of people he had never met or spoken a word to made me sick. I also immediately became conscious of my friend sitting next to me. You see, my friend has a few piercings and multiple tattoos, many of which are visible. He was also a member of that church.

Religious people can be mean and even heartless at times. That's just the way it is. Jesus, on the other hand, is full of love and grace. People need to see more of Jesus in those of us who claim to follow Him.

I recently received the following email from my missionary friend in Guatemala. He shared another sad but true story about how religion has failed those in desperate need:

This morning, a young man, 25 years old, knocked on our door for about 30 minutes straight. When we finally answered, there stood Daniel Gonzalez. He nervously explained his situation.

He did not want to come to our house today, but some friends had convinced him that it was his last chance. He said he was not the type of person to ask for things, so he was sorry for coming. He explained that yesterday, he had lost his home in a fire. A husband and father of 2 young kids, they had lost almost everything... house, bed, clothes, TV, food, and belongings - all ashes.

We were his last hope. I am thankful for that much—just being here, able to be that hope for somebody. That hope has a name—Jesus, and it is always amazing to me that we can "be" Jesus...

Now to the frustrating part. Why exactly were we his "last" hope?

Before showing up at our house, Daniel had exhausted his options. Most alarming was the response from his church from whom he was misled regarding "God's justice."

Rewind just 2 months to when Daniel and his wife Martha lost their 3rd child. Following childbirth, Florcita (little flower) spent 20 days on life support. Born two months premature, she hung on for 3 weeks before letting go. Daniel spent all 20 days & nights in the hospital at his wife's side, praying for Florcita to pull through.

Following their daughter's death, they returned to their church. Daniel, who was striving to become a deacon and took seriously his role collecting the weekly offering, was put on "probation" for missing 3 Sunday mornings and several other gatherings. He was told that missing church for any reason is a sin and requires discipline from the church authorities.

Now, after losing his house and all his belongings in the fire, the "church authority" explained to Daniel that God is righteous, punishing them for missing a few church services while clinging bedside to their dying daughter. The only effort to bring comfort was a simple reminder of the story of Job and how God won't give you more than you can handle.

After being denied by his church for help, they decided to try another church, this one well-known for helping the people of his neighborhood. This specific church has been working in his neighborhood for years, even recently completing a new community center to better serve them.

Martha returned home with the news. The church said there is nothing they can do because they only help families in the community who are members of their church.

Broken, denied, and ready to give up, he knocked on our door.

When we showed up at the site of their house this afternoon, Daniel made small talk for about 5-10 minutes. He was cheerful, seemed thrilled actually to see us. When he introduced us to his kids and showed us the extent of their remaining belongings, he got quieter, clearly trying to hide some emotion.

When he shared about the response from the churches, he broke. Confused and hurt, he began sobbing. It wasn't the loss of his daughter or his house that brought on the sobbing. It was the pain inflicted from the "church" that ultimately crushed him.

The very thing that is supposed to bring life, support, love, help, and hope… was killing him.

I wondered to myself if Daniel's pastor who avoided helping (but reminded Daniel about God's justice and Job's sufferings) had forgotten, or ever read, where Jesus said to love your neighbor as yourself. Paul's teachings about carrying one another's burdens also came to mind.

I also wondered how, as members of the same body of Jesus Christ, we could possibly deny help to those who aren't "members" of our own little private congregations.

But as we prayed, grace and hope started replacing the anger that was raging inside me. As frustrating as the pious, prosperity-blessing, false religion that poisons this culture is, in this moment God was giving us another opportunity to demonstrate His grace.

We prayed that this time of suffering would somehow bring freedom and set them free from the bondage of legalism. I hope that as we love on them, they will experience the real Jesus, His grace, and His Church.

The harsh reality is that religion can be heartless, cold and dead. Jesus, however, brings love and life to all who trust and follow Him. I am happy to say that the next day, someone from our spiritual community read this email and committed to raise the money to build a new house for this family.

James, the brother of Jesus, had some poignant words about religion. I really like the way *The Message Bible* conveys his thoughts.

"Anyone who sets himself up as 'religious' by talking a good game is self-deceived. This kind of religion is hot air and only hot air. *Real religion, the kind that passes muster before God the Father, is this: Reach out to the homeless and loveless in their plight, and guard against corruption from the godless world"* (James 1:26-27).

In other words, now is the time for the Church to do less talking and stop pointing fingers. Maybe we need to put down the stones and begin to come alongside those in need, just as Jesus did.

To be honest, I have pretty much given up on religion as we know it. However, my hope and trust is fully in *Jesus* Who is alive and working by His Spirit in the lives of people who know and follow Him all over the world. My desire is to walk with those who, like Jesus, will come alongside people in need and show them the love and compassion of God in the midst of their pain and struggle.

I find myself in agreement with Martin Luther King, Jr. when he said, "Perhaps I must turn my faith to the inner spiritual church, the church within the church, as the true ekklesia and the hope of the world." [13]

---

[13] King, Martin Luther, Jr. Letter From A Birmingham Jail. 16 April 1963. http://web.cn.edu/kwheeler/documents/Letter_Birmingham_Jail.pdf.

| CHAPTER SIX |

Steeple Envy

The beautiful people, the beautiful people, it's all relative to the size of your steeple.
--- Marilyn Manson from the song "The Beautiful People"

Does size matter? Is bigger really better? I guess it depends on who you ask and in what context you ask the question. For instance, when it comes to baseball, some would argue that the size of the bat is very important; others would say that it is not so much the size of the bat that matters but rather how well one can swing it. So maybe the answer is not as straightforward as some might think.

What about when it comes to church? Does size matter? Are we to believe that bigger is inherently better, and if one's steeple or congregation is large, then that church is successful? Conversely, does that mean if the church is small, then it's less successful, and the ability for it to make an impact must be small as well?

This may sound like a childish way of putting it, but entertain me for a moment here. As a pastor, I have experienced countless exchanges that went something like this: "Nice to meet you. What church are you with? How are things going? How many are you running these days?"

Of course, the first two questions are simply obligatory precursors to get to the third. Now think about this and tell me why that is so important to us. Why do we need to know if someone else has more or less people at their church than we do at ours? Could it be...steeple envy? [14]

We experience this kind of competition in different situations all through life. Men in particular are always comparing themselves to each other. Have you ever gone into a "real gym" where the real men work out? Good night! There are more mirrors than walls! Everyone wants to be the biggest dude in the place, and guys like me don't dare take off their shirts.

My son, Victor, is nine and I can't tell you how many times I've heard him complain about the fact that one of his little friends has a bigger Lego collection or more Star Wars figures than he does. And then there is Jonathan, my four-year old, who cries at times because he wants to be big like Victor. He wants all the stuff that Victor has, and he wants to do the things that Victor does. It's a never-ending, vicious cycle.

So my theory goes something like this: boys grow up to be men who continue this same competitive behavior. Inevitably, they find themselves comparing their lives to others. They look at what they have and what their friends have, and it's not much different than when they were kids. Only now, they're comparing their adult selection of toys, such as houses, cars, boats and 401k's. He who has the most toys wins, right?

Then there are boys who grow up and feel a certain calling to serve God and be in the ministry. Should we then be surprised when some of these guys follow suit? They do the same things but in a different context. Now they compare people, buildings and budgets.

Men and women alike share this competitive nature, and I don't believe that it's inherently bad or evil. In effect, when channeled correctly, it can be extremely healthy and positive. We've made many advances in areas such as technology and medicine because of this innate nature. There is something inside of us that doesn't like to lose, and so we fight to win. I think this is great when it comes to curing cancer or the myriad of great inventions that we have enjoyed as a result. I'm just not sure that the same holds true when it comes to the

---

[14] I want to give credit where credit is due. The "Isn't She Beautiful Conference" at Mars Hill was where I first heard the term "steeple envy" used. Rob Bell mentioned the quote from Marilyn Manson and talked about how pastors often compare themselves and their churches to one another.

world of ministry and church.

Jesus seemed to have turned this concept upside-down in much of His teaching. Apparently, there was an incident where He saw this very trait among His friends and followers. Look at how Jesus addressed the situation...

"They came to Capernaum. When He was in the house, He asked them, 'What were you arguing about on the road?' But they kept quiet because on the way they had argued about who was the greatest. Sitting down, Jesus called the Twelve and said, 'If anyone wants to be first, he must be the very last, and the servant of all'" (Mark 9:33-35).

WAS JESUS A FAILURE?

Throughout the Bible, winning often looked like losing. Jesus' own life was a perfect example of this. If you were to base the impact of His earthly ministry solely on the number of people who followed Him while He walked the earth, you would have to categorize Him as a complete failure. Sure, there were times when He had thousands who listened to Him. However, at the end of His life, He was basically deserted by everyone. Even His closest friends abandoned Him, and one of them betrayed Him with a kiss.

We all know that the story didn't end there. That's because we can look back on it from a historical perspective. But in the moment, you would have had to conclude that Jesus was a failure. Still, things were going on behind the scenes that were not understood until much later. He died, but then He rose. After showing Himself to His friends and followers, they later believed. Even the resurrection only resulted in 120 believers initially. Nonetheless, this small group was used to turn the world upside-down (or right-side-up) with His message.

What I'm getting at is how crazy it is that in church, we judge success to a large degree by bodies and buildings. Jesus didn't seem too concerned about how many people were following Him. What He was concerned about was doing what pleased His Father. He was challenged by the religious leaders for not following the status quo and doing what they thought was right. On one occasion, Jesus responded by saying, "I tell you the truth. The Son can do nothing by Himself; He can do only what He sees His Father doing, because whatever the Father does the Son also does." [15]

Later in John 6:38, we see that He responded similarly, "For I have come down from heaven not to do My will but to do the will of Him Who sent Me."

Jesus didn't bow down to popular opinion but rather sought to hear and do the Father's will. We have come to a place where we assume God's desires for us: a big church with all the programs that people think they need and a big building to house it all. I think we all know what can happen when you assume something. Could we be the butt of the joke (pun intended) because we've taken it upon ourselves to assume God's will in this instead of seeking it?

As a result, we view big churches as the most successful and will do whatever it takes to get there because obviously bigger is better. The goal has become growth, but that doesn't seem to line up with Jesus' goal. I just can't imagine Jesus hanging a sign outside His office door that reads, *"What is our business? Who is our customer? What does the customer consider to be of value?"* (I can't even imagine Jesus having an office.) But this is exactly what was found hanging outside the office of one of the most influential evangelical pastors in America.

So we do all kinds of things to get people in the doors. There are churches that don't talk about certain things on Sunday morning because they don't want to make un-churched people uncomfortable. Then there are churches whose services mimic that of a rock concert, complete with fog, moving lights and the whole nine yards. (Just for the record, I love a good rock show.) Finally, we have come to the point where some have resorted to crazy gimmicks to try to draw in people.

Below are some examples of what churches have done in their attempts to draw a crowd:

• A church in Alaska offered prizes in the form of airline certificates to those who brought the most guests to church over the Easter weekend. The values ranged from $500 for the *Passion of the Christ* movie on Good Friday, to $1,000 for the Easter morning service.

---

[15] John 5:19.

• A youth group recently staged a *Fear Factor*-type event which prompted an article titled "Peanut Butter Salvation" in a local paper. The subtitle said it all: "Why a Southside MegaChurch Thinks That Goldfish Swallowing and Toe-Licking Will Lead The Next Generation To God." After watching a video and hearing about the kids being dared to lick peanut butter off the toes of a youth leader, one parent commented, "It's inappropriate anywhere, but that it's happening in a church is just horrible. What would you think if that was happening in a home?"

The article then stated, "The mother suggests that the act between a minor and an adult in a private home would seem not only inappropriate, but perverse—and possibly illegal." [16]

• Another ploy is to use shock value or "creativity" to draw in people. That's what a pastor who once titled his personal blog, "Thoughts from one of this century's most intriguing and inspiring leaders and pastors" recently decided to do. During a sermon series on sex, he challenged married couples to have sex for seven days in a row. Now I have to admit, if you want to get guys in church, that will do it!

The sermon was advertised as "Seven Days of Sex" and was to be delivered from a bed. This stunt received a lot of publicity as the pastor was interviewed by CBS and other news outlets.[17] I love one blogger's comment. "I guess it's cool on the one hand that he's 'progressive.' But is it really, though? I think this is the same level of cool that the emo kids who hang at starbucks have, or even the guys with Mohawks who wear abercrombie." [18]

• One church gave away $8,000 in 3-D televisions, Nintendo game systems, movie tickets and other items to try to get people to attend their Easter service. I think this quote from the pastor explains the

---

[16] Susan Cooper Eastman. "Peanut Butter Salvation: Why A Southside MegaChurch Thinks That Goldfish Swallowing And Toe-Licking Will Lead The Next Generation To God." Folio Weekly September 2009. 01 October 2009. www.folioweekly.com/documents/main092909_001.pdf

[17] "Pastor's Sex Challenge." Narr. Julie Chen. CBS News, 2009. Web. 18 June 2011. www.cbsnews.com/stories/2008/11/13/earlyshow/living/relationships/main4598299.shtml

[18] Samuel Holder, "Sex sells church marketing," www.samseye.com, www.samseye.com/blog/files/6c60a423cdb931ba9302179d8519bb1f-1.html, 11 Dec. 2008.

intention well: "I have no problem with bribing people with crap in order to meet Christ." [19]

Is this what the church has come to, bribing people to fill our "buildings?"

Really?

Steeple envy is everywhere. Who has the most people? What church has the biggest building? Whose budget is bigger? How many staff members do you have? Are you multi-site? If so, how many?

Alright boys, get out your rulers...

It's competition at its worst.

So why does someone like Marilyn Manson see the problem, which he identifies and writes about in an awful song about Christians, and all the church people just turn a blind eye to it? Why do we allow the competition and coveting to continue? How can we get so caught up in such things that we miss the forest for the trees, and our buildings become more important than people?

Some churches and pastors care so much about their reputations that they probably wouldn't even let someone like Marilyn Manson walk through the doors of their beautiful edifice. Most religious people would say, "That's not true. Those are the people we want here, the ones who really need Jesus." That sounds really good because it's the right thing to say. But that's not always reality.

Consider a true story about a very influential church that happens to be located in the downtown portion of their city. They have a multi-million dollar complex that spans multiple city blocks, and they claim somewhere in the neighborhood of 20,000 members. (That's one big steeple.)

Since this church's location is in the downtown area of the city, homeless people showing up there is not unusual. This has happened so often that they have trained their uniformed security (yes, they have uniforms and look like police officers) how to handle these situations.

Homeless people have walked into this church on many occasions

[19] *Metro church bribes worshippers with electronics.* Narr. Boua Xiong. KARE11, 2011. Kare11.com. Web. http://www.kare11.com/rss/article/920199/391/Metro-church-bribes-worshippers-with-electronics. 22 April 2011.

only to be escorted out by security. This is common knowledge. I'm sure they're kind when they tell them in the most loving way that they're not welcome there. But tell me God doesn't weep when things like this happen. And then try to tell those who are on the outside-looking-in that Jesus isn't like that. The obvious question is, "If Jesus isn't like that, then why is the church like that?"

Although this may be an extreme example, it is a real story, and similar incidents happen throughout churches all over America. Certain people are treated with a degree of respect and dignity based on how they look, what kind of car they drive, or more importantly, how much they give. While others may not be shown the door like those homeless people, they certainly are not given the same attention, and they get less face-to-face time with the pastor than the more affluent.

This occurs all the time. I don't think anyone addresses this issue better than James, the brother of Jesus. Listen to what he had to say:

"My brothers, as believers in our glorious Lord Jesus Christ, don't show favoritism. Suppose a man comes into your meeting wearing a gold ring and fine clothes, and a poor man in shabby clothes also comes in. If you show special attention to the man wearing fine clothes and say, 'Here's a good seat for you,' but say to the poor man, 'You stand there' or 'Sit on the floor by my feet,' have you not discriminated among yourselves and become judges with evil thoughts?" (James 2:1-4).

Those were pretty strong words that James used. I'm glad that they're his words and not mine. I would actually say something simple like, "People shouldn't judge by appearance. That really stinks that people do that." But he went much farther and said, "You have discriminated...and become judges with evil thoughts."

I particularly remember when our little Bible study group talked about this passage while going through the book of James, verse-by-verse. I was so moved by what I read that I was compelled to make the following statement: "If you are a person of means and feel like a pastor or church leader (this includes me) is giving you extra attention or preferential treatment, I would like to give you this piece of advice—run! Run as fast as you can and as far as you can from that place. From what James said, that person is judging with 'evil thoughts,' and I would never suggest that you submit yourself or your family to that kind of spiritual leader."

Why does James use such strong words here? What is so evil about that person's actions? The answer may seem simple, but I think that this person's actions reveal his or her motives, which stem from a deeper issue—one of control.

What happens is that leaders within the church often begin to usurp the position of God. They somehow come to the point where they believe that their job is to now make sure the ministry succeeds. In reality and as I understand it from the Bible, their job has more to do with sharing the good news of Jesus with people and equipping them for service in His Kingdom and less to do with the marketing and growing of the church. And last I checked, God has promised to take care of the rest.

I think part of the problem is that pastors feel like they're supposed to build this thing called "the church." But that's not really their responsibility. Jesus said, "I will build My Church, and the gates of Hades will not overcome it." Jesus has committed to build the Church.

So whose church is it?

Is it the pastor's church, or is it Jesus' Church? Whose smiling face is in the church bulletin and on the website? Who have the marketing consultants said we must use to brand the church and place on billboards and put in newspaper ads?

Really. Whose church is it?

In many instances, the pastor seems to have "majority ownership" of the church. I have come to believe that this may be the single most fundamental problem we see in the American church today.

Many churches are personality-driven as opposed to mission-driven, and Jesus no longer possesses full ownership. He has become a silent partner of sorts Who answers to the pastor's wishes and desires. He is called upon to provide money when it's time to build the new building but rarely consulted as to whether or not a new building is really the best option at the time.

Now I know that pastors pray to Jesus before their meetings with the marketing team and before they meet with those that they have hired to handle the capital campaign. My question is whether or not we're taking the time to ask Jesus if we really need a marketing team or a capital campaign. I know that a lot of churches have them, but does that make it right? Haven't a lot of parents told their kids, "Just because everyone is doing it doesn't mean it's the right thing to do." Maybe we should take our parents' advice on this one and ask more questions before taking the bait, hook, line and sinker.

Let's be honest. If the goal was to get the biggest crowd, then Jesus really wasn't that good of a leader. He must not have learned that He was supposed to launch large and do all the things that make people comfortable to keep them coming around. He didn't leave behind any giant buildings with a wing or gymnasium dedicated in His name or anything like that.

Instead, He taught about the Kingdom of God, a place where things almost seemed upside-down compared to this earthly kingdom. He challenged people to not only love their neighbor, but to love their enemy. Jesus didn't accept religious elitism. He made sure that the religious leaders knew they were no better in God's eyes than the sinners who they had marginalized and kept at arm's length. He told people that there was more to life than what meets the eye. He talked about another Kingdom beyond what we can see and said that was the place where we should store up treasures and invest our lives and time.

I think about that and then listen to the messages that come from many pulpits today. I wonder if Jesus would even be accepted in many of our churches. Are we as concerned with God's Kingdom as Jesus was? Or do we spend most of our time, energy and money on things that have more to do with this earthly kingdom?

A book that recently had a deep impact on me was *Crazy Love* by Francis Chan. He has a chapter titled "Your Best Life Later," and I love it! Why? Because it sounds more like Jesus than a lot of the self-help, prosperity-now messages we hear today.

Let me set the record straight and say that I don't think there is anything wrong with having a big church. I actually think a large church is great as long as it's functioning in such a way that the mission of God is central, and people are experiencing authentic community. We find ourselves in trouble when the goal of growing takes precedent over Kingdom priorities.

ONE CHURCH

I don't think that size matters much to God, and I really don't think it should matter nearly as much as it does to most pastors. I believe that the house church of 10 or 20 people can be just as legitimate an expression of God's Church as a gathering of 1,000 or 20,000. I don't think God necessarily sees one as more significant than the other. In fact, maybe God sees them as one in the same, assuming that in each case, the church is a reproducing, mission-focused community of believers.

Paul talked about the Church being a body made up of many parts and that no one part was more significant than another. Actually, he said that the parts should show concern for one another. If one part of the body hurts or suffers, then the whole body suffers. What if we viewed the "body" as being God's Church and saw all of these individual congregations as parts of that one body working together to accomplish something great for God?

I know that we normally read this passage and see "the body" as the local congregation and the individual parts as the members of that body. But could this apply to the larger context of the Church as well? Maybe God doesn't care about the size of individual congregations because He looks down, and in reality, sees only *One Church*. I think most Christians would agree that every person who genuinely knows and follows Jesus is a part of *the Church*. When we gather, I will often ask the question, "How many churches are there in Jacksonville?" And I am happy to say that the immediate response from the crowd is, "One!" Does God only see one Church? Think of the implications.

If every believer were seen as a part of the same church, then none of us would have any right to lay claim to "our church." If it is

His Church, then He gets all the glory. Who has the most people or the biggest building isn't important. If it is His Church, do we have the right to get so bent out of shape when someone chooses to leave and attend somewhere else? If we believed that the Church actually belongs to God, then we can be confident that He will provide for its needs. No longer would there be the need for gimmicks to draw people or coercion to get people to give.

Then maybe we would stop with the competition. Maybe then we would be able to work together to show Jesus' love to the world in tangible ways which they could understand. Herein may lie the answer to Jesus' prayer for the disciples and those of us who would believe as a result of their message:

"'My prayer is not for them alone (the disciples). I pray also for those who will believe in Me through their message, that all of them may be one, Father, just as You are in Me and I am in You. May they also be in Us so that the world may believe that You have sent Me'" (John 17:20-21).

There is a world that needs to believe, and there is a church that needs to be united. Jesus made it clear that the two are not mutually exclusive. Furthermore, He saw the unity of believers to be so crucial that He took time to specifically pray for this to happen; He then left a written record for us to consider. His evident desire for His body to come together as one should be enough for us to put down our rulers and be willing to work together for the greater good.

"'A new command I give you: Love one another. As I have loved you, so you must love one another. By this all men will know that you are My disciples, if you love one another'" (John 13:34-45).

Chapter Seven

Video Killed the Radio Star

I have to admit, I'm an '80s child. And what do I have to show for it? Well, I can probably beat most of you in foosball and air hockey, and I remember thinking Pong was the coolest game ever made. Also, I'm one of a select few who can say they competed in the original Donkey Kong, Pac Man and Asteroids tournaments.

As a teenager, I experienced the genesis of cable TV. Does anyone else remember those set-top boxes with the clicker knob for the original 20 or 30 cable channels that were available back then? One of those channels was MTV, which by the way, actually showed music videos. Martha Quinn and Nina Blackwood were the eye candy, I mean VJ's, who hosted the show and kept all the teenage boys glued to the screen.

The year was 1981, and I remember tuning in regularly to get my fix of Devo, Pat Benatar, Rod Stewart, and believe it or not, U2. The first three makes me feel a bit old, but throw U2 in the mix, and I feel halfway hip. Actually, if you want to get a little laugh, check out U2's video "I Will Follow," which aired that year. The new-wave Bono is a little different than the larger-than-life rock star who we know today. (Still good stuff though.)

I also remember the very first video to ever air on MTV. Any other '80s children or Trivial Pursuit geeks who are able to recall what it was? Wait for it............

"Video Killed The Radio Star" by The Buggles.

Can you think of a better chorus to introduce the newest format of music? Sing it with me: "*Video killed the radio star. Video killed the ra-*

dio star. In my mind and in my car, we can't rewind. We've gone too far..." Pretty catchy tune and quite appropriate for the occasion.

Which brings me to the question,

When it comes to church, have we gone too far?

A few years ago, I took my first trip to California. Roxane and I were celebrating our 15-year anniversary, so we took the opportunity to travel from L.A. up the Pacific Coast Highway to see the giant redwoods. Breathtaking. We took our time and soaked it all in. We would drive for awhile and then stop to see things, like sea lions sunning themselves on the sand. We also stopped to hang out in Santa Barbara, which is a place that everyone should visit at least once.

After coming back into the L.A. area, we made another stop. I'll never forget rolling up on this crazy glass structure with mirrors that reflected the sun like nothing you have ever seen. It was quite the steeple. Maybe you've seen it on TV. That's right, the Crystal Cathedral. It's a beautiful glass building with walls that move electronically and all kinds of cool stuff. They even have an outdoor Biblical museum filled with statues and gardens.

What stood out to me more than everything else was the drive-in. No kidding. They have their own outdoor drive-in theater of sorts. Apparently when Robert Schuller first started the church, the people met in a drive-in theater. So when they built the Crystal Cathedral in 1961, they decided to preserve this aspect of the church. The building was made in such a way that at the push of a button, these giant 25-foot glass doors would open. Schuller could preach not only to the crowd inside but also to those in cars in the parking lot. The theater appeared to still be functional, with a giant screen and designated places to park so that you can watch and listen from your car.

I have to admit that I laughed as I thought about its absurdity. Drive-in church? Are you kidding me? This led to a string of questions in my mind. For instance, I couldn't help but wonder if the Crystal Cathedral had a night service. And if so, did Rev. Schuller ever preach on the Song of Solomon? That could make for an interesting church experience for some.

I also wondered how they handled some of the regular church practices. For instance, how is the offering received? Was there a credit card swipe somewhere? Or maybe it was more like going to Sonic. I could just picture some ladies rolling up on skates, carrying the offering baskets and communion trays. Do you have to tip them, or do they get a percentage from the kitty?

Seriously though, this whole concept of the drive-in church made me think a little bit more about what the church really is and what it has become. As we have seen, the Church throughout the New Testament was a gathered group of people. It was never referred to as a place. The people lived in community with one another as God had intended. They knew and prayed for each other. When someone had a need, they helped each other. Together they were to emulate the love of Jesus to the world as they lived out their faith and served those in need around them.

So how can something like that happen in the world of "drive-in church?" You arrive in your car—alone—or with your family. You watch the service and listen to it—alone—in your car. If you sing, I guess you do that alone in your car as well. This would make every Sunday similar to one of those Chevy Chase vacation moments when you're in the family truckster singing. Then you leave—alone—in your car.

If you did this week-in and week-out, could you define that as Biblical Church? This practice seems outlandish, but actually it's not that different from what thousands of people do every Sunday in America. They walk into a huge crowded building—alone. They watch, listen and sing—alone. And ultimately, they leave—alone—only to return the next week to do it all over again. That might be church in America today, but it certainly cannot be characterized as the Church of the New Testament.

I also began to wonder if Robert Schuller was the forerunner to the ever-so-popular multi-site, video-venue phenomenon in America? I would guess that a lot of pastors might like to distance themselves from this thought.

For anyone who might not be familiar with this concept, a multi-site church is simply one church that meets in multiple locations. The different venues could be anywhere from a movie theatre or a school to a bar or restaurant. However, it maintains a central structure, central leadership, etc. This expression of church is becoming more and more popular and appears to be an effective way of reaching people in some contexts.

One model for a multi-site church involves showing a live stream or prerecorded message that's given by the pastor at the central campus. Everything else is live, such as the music, and of course, the offering; the message is then beamed-in from the mother ship. Each campus will usually have mini-pastors on staff who help manage things and run the "show." Forgive me for my cynicism.

I know this movement is the hot new trend, and I realize that I'm venturing into an area that will probably cost me some potential friends. That's OK. The whole reason I'm writing this book is to share my mind and heart without being influenced by what people think or how they'll react. Surely I'm not the first to have these thoughts, although I may be one of the few to put these questions on the printed page.

I understand that when a church becomes wildly popular and encounters significant growth, some people want to duplicate the experience. In a way, that makes sense to me. I mean, duplication happens every day in the business world, which is why we have chains of specific stores and restaurants. But are we selling burgers here?

A friend of mine who was on staff at one of the fastest growing churches in America gave me a little insight to the multi-site church. This church functions with a central campus where the pastor teaches live. The sermons are recorded on a DVD and then played at the church's numerous campuses.

The concept was often described in staff meetings as a franchise just like Starbucks or anything else. When people enter these places, they have certain expectations. Therefore, the idea is to give people the same experience in another location. "We have to reproduce the (insert church name here) experience," my friend told me.

I understand the basic concept of this, but to me, this thinking seems flawed. First of all, Starbucks as well as every other franchise or chain is a business, and they're selling products and services. In those settings, people do have these expectations, and that's normal. Does that really transfer into the church world?

I recently spoke with an old friend who is on the pastoral staff of a growing church in the mid-west. He told me that his church had grown considerably and that they were looking to expand its ministry. The plan was to form a multi-site model; they would plant a church in another area by using a video venue. The music would be live, and the pastor's message would be delivered via video.

He was wrestling with this idea and wanted to talk to someone. He was very positive about the ministry of the church but was beginning to feel like it was becoming somewhat personality-driven. This wasn't setting well with him. He shared with me a discussion they had in one of their staff meetings, which we both found a bit disturbing. Someone apparently made the statement that all they needed to do was put together the right band and show a video of their pastor and they would be guaranteed success, since they would be the "best show in town."

Has the church been reduced to this? Just put on the best show and success is now guaranteed? Once again, we have to ask ourselves how we define "success" in God's Kingdom? Are we successful if we draw the biggest crowd?

Don't get me wrong. I think innovation is good. I'm all for being as creative as possible in order to get the message of Jesus to those who normally might not be reached. The best way to get started in some situations may even be the use of a video service. I just don't believe that this is a sustainable model, and I have a hard time reconciling it with what I read in the Bible. Why not be willing to raise up leaders who would one day be able to use their God-given gifts to teach and pastor the church?

Has pursuing excellence and creativity, both of which are good things, superseded our dependence on the power of God? I think about the words the Apostle Paul wrote to the believers in Corinth:

"When I came to you, brothers, I did not come with eloquence or superior wisdom as I proclaimed to you the testimony about God. For I resolved to know nothing while I was with you except Jesus Christ and Him crucified. I came to you in weakness and fear, and with much trembling. My message and my preaching were not with wise and persuasive words, but with a demonstration of the Spirit's power, so that your faith might not rest on men's wisdom, but on God's power" (1 Corinthians 2:1-5).

I could be wrong, but I don't think Paul would have been a good candidate for a multi-site church set-up. According to history, he wasn't a very attractive guy, so he wouldn't have been very camera-friendly. He also didn't seem to have many of the qualities that would have attracted crowds. Evidently, his preaching was quite simple—Jesus Christ and Him crucified.

I also find it hard to envision Paul, or any of the disciples for that matter, spending large amounts of time and money to produce elaborate stage set-ups for their upcoming sermon series. Imagine the conversation, "How about we do the backdrop like the prison where Silas and I were thrown in after being beaten with rods? That would be awesome!" Maybe it's just me, but I find the thought of this image laughable.

Paul was the kind of guy who was more interested in sharing the love of Jesus with people and making disciples. He would then trust God to carry-on the work with other leaders who were raised up. It wasn't his Church. It belonged to Jesus, and apparently he was willing to trust Him with it.

Now don't get me wrong. I'm not saying the multi-site video model isn't effective in some ways. It definitely can be used to draw a crowd, and life change can take place in this context. But once that happens, why not hand off the church to someone who is called and gifted to pastor God's people? Could it be another case of steeple envy?

The reality is that the turn-over rate of campus pastors in these situations is quite high. Many of them only last in the role for a short season and then go on to plant their own churches or to pastor existing congregations. As a matter of fact, I know of a large multi-site church that has unintentionally planted three churches in the last three years by having campus pastors leave.

I think there are other variations of multi-site churches that are very creative and more sustainable. Some use a preaching team that rotates from campus to campus. Others have on-site pastors who actually preach and teach, but the vision of the church comes from the main campus, and they share offices in a central location.

"Video may have killed the radio star" in the '80s. However, I'm simply not convinced that the video stars within the church today will outlast those who give their heart and soul to people for the sake of the gospel.

Labeling this new phenomenon as anything other than a form of personality-driven ministry is difficult. Historically, personality-driven ministries have been less sustainable than missional or mission-driven ministries. Besides, the Bible doesn't seem to support this model in any way.

The mission of Jesus will remain until this world comes to an end. People, though, come and go. The reality is that people get old and eventually die, not to mention those who disqualify themselves from the ministry. Therefore, ministries that are centered more on a person rather than the mission of Jesus are vulnerable and less sustainable.

Remember Robert Schuller? He is now retired and only preaches occasionally at the Crystal Cathedral. Unfortunately in October of 2010, the ministry was forced to file Chapter 11 Bankruptcy, citing the decline in donations and a $48 million debt as the causes.

Let us all hope and pray that the bankruptcy of Schuller's ministry is not a sign of things to come and that the words to "Video Killed the Radio Star" do not prove to be prophetic in any way.

"...In my mind and in my car, we can't rewind. We've gone too far..."

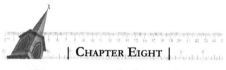

CHAPTER EIGHT

Funny Undies

To be completely honest, I had no idea what I was going to do after my "holy crap" moment. As I have said, I wasn't too excited about the church, and I had seen enough to make me as jaded as the next person. In fact, I had seen it all from the inside. The people who were supposed to be closest to God were some of the people who were causing me to question the church. I was beginning to wonder if God was really in the institutional church at all. Then I remembered what first drew me to Jesus and those who followed Him.

Love.

My life was radically changed in college when I decided to follow Jesus. I went from a destructive life of alcoholism, drug abuse and immorality to passionately following Jesus and genuinely enjoying life. I found a group of people who weren't perfect, nor did they claim to be, but they were on the same spiritual journey as me. The only way to describe our relationship is that we enjoyed a beautiful sense of community unlike anything I had ever had. Call me naïve, but I expected these kinds of relationships and experiences to continue throughout my journey.

Like many others, I have been disappointed along the way. I certainly have built some meaningful, deep relationships within the church, which unfortunately have been the exception and not the norm. I find this a bit curious. In the book of Acts, we see a Church that was filled with people who were committed to God and to one another. It was a spiritual family of sorts.

Have you ever experienced this kind of community among a group of people? I think that many of us probably have on some level. But for most of us, it was probably outside the confines of the church. My first memory of this sense of community was with a small group of friends when I was growing up. We did everything together, so much so that we shared a sense of family. Granted, we got in all kinds of trouble, and our group was unhealthy in many ways. However, one thing was for sure—we were there for each other.

Recently, I was humorously reminded of another event in life that brought this sense of community. I was helping a few guys put a roof on a friend's house. His roof had been leaking for a while, and he didn't have the funds to fix it, so our church decided to help by paying for the new roof. We believed that Jesus wouldn't want little children to have to live in a house that "cries," which is how this man's son described the water that was leaking into his bedroom.

Because of another obligation, I was only able to stay for a little while. Seeing a group of guys helping a brother in need was a beautiful sight, not to mention I got a real good laugh in the process.

Since I only had a short window of time, I tried to get right to work. We were putting on a metal roof, so screwing it down was a big part of the job. Hundreds of screws were needed to secure the roof, so I got my hands on a drill and went at it.

I wasn't long into the job when my buddy Carl came up behind me, laughing. He asked under his breath, "Hey, does that say, "'Ozzy?'"

I immediately knew what he was referring to, so I proceeded to stand up and pull my pants up to my waist. This accomplished two things. First, it took away any resemblance that I might have to a plumber. And second, it hid my tattoo which apparently had begun to show.

Carl continued to laugh. He then said, "Seriously, you never told me that you had "Ozzy" tattooed on your..."

By this time, I had begun to laugh as well. Everyone else was trying to figure out what was so funny. I discreetly assured him that I didn't have a tattoo that said, "Ozzy." It actually said, "I.O. 633 Cooch" across the top, which is what he must have begun to see.

We had a pretty good laugh while everyone around us was oblivious to what was so funny. Carl, being a good dude and not wanting to embarrass me, didn't let on for a minute as to what he saw, or thought that he saw for that matter.

After I left, one of the other guys came up to him and asked, "What was so funny? Did Vic have some funny underwear on or something?"

Carl, trying to keep his composure, responded, "Well, kind of."

That led to the next horrific but hilarious question. "What was it? A thong or something?"

Carl could have really thrown me under the bus at this point, but thankfully, he didn't. He simply laughed. "No," he said, "it wasn't that bad," and left it at that.

So to put an end to any rumors about funny underwear, let me say it loud and not so proud, "It was a tattoo!"

So why does a man get a tattoo on his butt cheek? Well, a mature man usually doesn't, but a young man might. I actually grew up with three brothers, two of which had multiple tattoos. I never liked tattoos and swore that I would never get one. And then I went to college.

While there, I joined a fraternity and did a lot of stupid things, one of which I'll carry with me until the day I die. Although this group was unhealthy in many ways, it did give me a legitimate sense of community at that time. We were a group of guys who may have been very misguided, but we were misguided together. There wasn't much that a guy wouldn't do for his "brother," and we certainly had each other's back.

Many of the guys lived together at the "frat" house. Those of us who didn't, found ourselves there day and night. We ate, drank and did most things together. We were a family of sorts. For some, it was a home away from home; for others, it was the closest thing to a real family that they had ever experienced. During this time of my life, this group was very significant to me.

A tradition had started a few years earlier. Those guys who were really dedicated got the fraternity crest tattooed on their right cheek, along with their nickname and scroll number. So one night after a little "liquid courage," my big brother JP and I took a ride to the tattoo parlor. And the rest is history.

Even if a community is centered on things that are destructive, it can still be very attractive and powerful. The environment may not be the most positive, but it still resonates deep in one's soul. The sense of community is real and often magnetic. Why? Because God created us to live in community. He desires for us to be interdependent as opposed to independent. Independence is an American thing, not a God thing. So if God created us this way, it seems logical that being a part of community would be compelling to us, so much so that we would even do crazy things just to be a part of such a group.

In his book *Forgotten God*, Francis Chan recounts a story about what happened to a gang member who came to his church:

A while back, a former gang member came to our church. He was heavily tattooed and rough around the edges, but he was curious to see what church was like. He had a relationship with Jesus and seemed to get fairly involved with the church.

After a few months, I found out the guy was no longer coming to the church. When asked why he didn't come anymore, he gave the following explanation: "I had the wrong idea of what church was going to be like. When I joined the church, I thought it was going to be like joining a gang. You see, in the gangs we weren't just nice to each other once a week – we were family." That killed me because I knew that what he expected is what the church is intended to be. It saddened me to think that a gang could paint a better picture of commitment, loyalty, and family than the local church body. [20]

The reality is that people should never be so desperate. True community should start within the context of a loving family environment. However, with the divorce rate around 50%, this is rarely the case. Many of us grow up looking for that feeling of love and acceptance elsewhere. And with the church becoming less personal and more institutional, we shouldn't be surprised that so many people are seeking this fulfillment elsewhere.

Christianity as we know it today is much more of a religious system than an invitation to truly know and love God. Religion can never sat-

[20] Francis Chan, *Forgotten God: Reversing Our Tragic Neglect of the Holy Spirit* (Colorado Springs: David C. Cook, 2009), 152.

isfy the deepest desires in one's soul, and true community cannot be experienced by becoming a member of an organization, including a church. Community is experienced as people share life together.

THE JOURNEY

So there I was with a few friends and their families, asking questions like, "What is the Church? What is it called to do? How does it function so that God's agenda overrides our personal agenda? And what would an expression of that look like today?"

At first we thought we would just get together, study the bible, sing and maybe pray because that's what you do at church, right? Then we realized that one of the components missing from our own church experience was authentic relationships. We all had church friends. But as some of us found out, they were only our friends if we went to church together or did the things that the church said we were supposed to do. We figured that God must want something more than that for his people.

We also noticed that throughout the pages of the Bible, eating seemed to be a big part of what the people of God did together. The Israelite community was centered on feasts and festivals. They celebrated three major feasts, and some of these were basically parties that lasted for eight days. Also, they were to participate in other numerous holy days and festivals that God had established for them.

So we decided that we would gather some friends, cook out and then read and discuss the Bible together. What a novel idea, hanging-out with one another around a table, eating and sharing life together. It almost felt like this was the way things ought to be. As we discovered and have already discussed earlier, this was common practice among the early Church.

"They devoted themselves to the apostles' teaching and to the fellowship, to the breaking of bread and to prayer. Everyone was filled with awe, and many wonders and miraculous signs were done by the apostles. All the believers were together and had everything in common. Selling their possessions and goods, they gave to anyone as he had need. Every day they continued to meet together in the temple courts. They broke bread in their homes and ate together with glad and sincere hearts, praising God and enjoying the favor of all the people. And the Lord added to their number daily those who were being saved" (Acts 2:42-47).

The early followers of Jesus were devoted to the apostles' teaching, the fellowship, the breaking of bread, and prayer. To them, these were the times and events that were most important and non-negotiable. They met together in the temple courts, which allowed for a larger group setting. They also broke bread in their homes. When they did these few simple things, God seemed to work among them in powerful ways.

We actually read through that passage together at one of our first gatherings and asked the question, "What was more important in the early Church, meeting in the temple courts in a larger group or breaking bread in each other's homes?"

In an effort to be true to what we read and after some discussion, we concluded that the two seemed equally important. As a result, we decided that we would view church in the same way. Yes, gathering together as a larger group was important. But equally important was the gathering in each other's homes and sharing life together in a more personal way.

What does this mean for the life of the church, and what does that look like? We seemingly have names for everything nowadays, along with strategies and formulas to match. So when you say that the small group gatherings in homes are as important as the large group gatherings, you're immediately categorized as a "cell church" or a church of small groups, etc.

We decided that we would attempt to go the route of the early Church and just make this a priority rather than a program. Therefore, we simply recognized the importance of smaller gatherings in homes and decided that we would make time and space for them to take place. Why crowd the calendar with more meetings? Let's gather together as a large group weekly, and then encourage people to break bread and share life together in various ways throughout the week.

This practice gave room for what some would consider a traditional small group Bible study. It also legitimized getting together with another couple to spend time sitting around a table and sharing a meal together. Sometimes the deepest conversations and most meaningful times are found in the natural setting of eating and doing life together. This is true for Christ-followers as well as for those who aren't following Jesus. Not everyone will come to a church gathering or a small group meeting, but virtually everyone you know will come over for dinner. As far as I can tell, God works in both settings, and both are equally spiritual with the same potential for life change and transformation.

So that's what we did. We grilled out, studied the Bible and got to know one another. It was refreshing. We had no hidden agenda and no need to feel like we had to grow in numbers. We didn't feel that we had to become anything other than a group of people who were trying to follow Jesus the best we knew how. That included those of us who were trying to lead and facilitate the gathering. We were sure to let everyone know that we were all on this journey together and that none of us had it figured out. In actuality, those of us who had been in church the longest may have had a disadvantage to those who were new to all of this.

Our little group didn't take long to grow beyond what our house could handle. Five couples soon became 10 and that meant a lot of kids as well. I think we had like 12 families and more than 20 kids on the night that my wife, Roxane, looked at me and said, "Alright. I'm about done!"

We had outgrown the setting of our house, which was becoming unmanageable. Thankfully, we had a clubhouse in our community and so did Dennis and Eve, our friends who helped lead the group at that time. We held our next few meetings at clubhouses and enjoyed that short season together as well.

Because of certain restrictions in our communities, we were only able to reserve places to meet for three more weeks. After that, we didn't know what we would do. So we began to pray.

I prayed, "Jesus, You said that You will build Your Church. Well this is Your Church, and it looks like Your Church needs a home. So if You want this to continue, You're going to have to do something." To my surprise, God answered those prayers in short order!

Through a mutual friend, we met a man named Andy, a follower of Jesus and a businessman in Jacksonville, Florida. I heard that he owned a building with a meeting place in it that just might work for us. Upon meeting him, he shared with us a story that blew us away.

Andy told us that he had received a dream from God about a year earlier. What he described was a literal dream like the ones you read about in the Bible. He said that in this dream, God showed him a facility that he was to build. It would be used as a place of worship and ministry to advance His Kingdom in Jacksonville. Andy had no desire to start a church or anything like that, but he was a man who loved God and wanted to follow Jesus.

So when Andy purchased a new building for his business, he was obedient and built the room that he saw in his dream. (You have to hear him tell the story.) He designed the room specifically as he had seen it and was just finishing the construction when we met him in March of 2007.

Words cannot describe what I felt when I walked into that room. The space was fully equipped with a stage, sound system, lights, high def TVs on the wall and about 100 chairs. Upon seeing the space and hearing his vision for the rest of the facility, which was unfinished at that time, I said, "Andy, I think you may have just built the meeting place for our church."

He replied, "No, I think God did because He told me to do it." I sat down and literally wept.

In this moment, I was reminded and convinced of the fact that God is still a God of miracles, even to this day. If there is something that God wants done, we shouldn't be surprised that He would do something crazy, like give direction in a dream to someone who would listen and obey.

While it appeared obvious that God had arranged this meeting to provide the place for our church to meet, I had one lingering question.

How would a small group of people pay for a facility when they had never even collected a single offering? Once again, we needed to pray. We were asking God for wisdom when Andy walked back into the auditorium where we were praying. He had come to let us know that he was going to try to reduce the cost of the facility as much as possible to help us. Although this was an answer to prayer, the real answer was yet to come.

Even with the cost reduction, we knew the facility was still going to stretch us beyond our comfort level. Andy then told us about the International Learning Center (ILC), an organization that was also interested in leasing the space but couldn't afford it. The director was "coincidentally" scheduled to be at the building in an hour. So we stayed and decided to hang out and meet her.

Upon meeting Kim and hearing about ILC's vision, we began to see the wisdom of God in this situation. They show the love of Christ to internationals within our community as they teach them English so that they can become fully functioning members of society.

We were then led to ask the question, "Why should we pay for a facility to be used a couple of days a week, only to remain empty the majority of the time? Why not share space and expenses and maximize God's resources?"

This idea made sense. It also gave us the opportunity to begin to practice what would become one of our core values: to partner with other churches and organizations in our city in order to join God in what He is doing.

As was said earlier, we had clubhouses reserved for three weeks, but we didn't know what we would do after that; so we cried out to God.

On the fourth week, we found ourselves meeting in a wonderful, fully-equipped facility with plenty of room for the kids! This facility would give us the opportunity to continue our dream, the dream that we could be the Church without feeling forced to do church the American way. We felt no pressure or distinct desire to grow numerically or become anything. We simply wanted to know and understand what it meant to love God first and foremost. We then wanted to share that love with our neighbors in meaningful, tangible ways like Jesus had commanded.

What you have just read is the testimony of what God did. We were on a journey together as a community. That journey has continued, and our little community has grown in unconventional ways.

| Chapter Nine |

Show Me The Money!

Let us more and more insist on raising funds of love, of kindness, of understanding, of peace. Money will come if we seek first the Kingdom of God—the rest will be given.

---*Mother Teresa*

Money is an enigma. You need money to survive, but falling in love with it can kill you. It makes the world go around, but money can't buy you love. Some people clutch it tightly while others burn through it faster than gasoline in a Hummer.

The reality is that money is necessary in order to function in our world. But we don't need to strive for money, nor does it need to be our focus. We are told that God owns everything. The Bible says that He owns the cattle on a 1,000 hills, and He has the ability to provide for our every need.[21] Yet fighting the allure of riches is difficult, and many of us chase the almighty dollar.

Unfortunately, self-indulgence and greed have permeated our culture to the point that they go unnoticed by the majority. The sad fact is that both self-serving traits have not only pervaded our culture but the church as well. The sense of entitlement that seems to be growing among evangelical Christians is very unsettling.

The assumption is that those who follow Jesus and lead His Church should also expect to achieve the American Dream in the process. This supposition is in stark contrast to what we see of Jesus and His followers in the New Testament. Jesus' message to His followers

[21]Psalm 50:10 and Matthew 6:33.

was one of sacrifice, and He encouraged them to be more concerned about storing-up treasure in heaven rather than here on earth. [22]

I don't believe this means that all who follow Jesus are called to a life of poverty. I do, however, struggle with this sense of entitlement that comes not only through messages preached but also through the lifestyles of those who deliver those messages. Based on the way most leaders within the church live, we shouldn't be surprised that there is little sign of sacrifice within the American church today.

Jesus, Peter and Paul clearly preached that this world is not our home and thus not worthy of us giving our lives to it.[23] We are called to live for another Kingdom, a Kingdom that will have no end and where all pain, suffering and injustice will one day cease to exist. Jesus said, "'Where your treasure is, there your heart will be also.'" [24]

So where is the "treasure" in most churches today?

Where is the "treasure" in those who lead the church?

Where is your "treasure?"

There you will find the heart.

Where we have our treasures is easily identified by looking at buildings and budgets. Making this determination is not rocket science. A cursory glance at how we spend our money will tell us where our heart is. Jesus said that our hearts should be in heaven. Therefore, heaven is where our treasure should be as well.

So how do we justify ministers receiving salaries similar to that of a pro athlete? Private jets are not uncommon for some of God's superstars. Mercedes-Benz's and even Bentley's are the cars of choice for some. A former staff member of a well-known mega-church in our country said that the Cadillac Escalade was jokingly referred to as the "staff limo" because so many of the staff drove one.

I know that this is an area that's supposed be off-limits for discussion or question. However, we have come to a place where the world looks at the church with a jaded eye, having little confidence in its spiritual leaders today. And I would say with good reason. We (I

---

[22]Matthew 6:19-24.
[23]Matthew 16:24-27, 1 Peter 1:17-21, and Philippians 1:21.
[24]Matthew 6:21.

used that word again) have lost their trust by doing stupid and asinine things. We just go on with business as usual, barely acknowledging all of the abuse, let alone trying to do anything to bring about change.

TRIBAL COUNCIL

I will never forget the story my friend shared with me shortly after his trip to the pastor's office to look at the church finances. There were some financial decisions made that had left him and his wife with some questions, which was what prompted their visit. In addition, the church had never disclosed any real details regarding its finances.

To me, his request to review the books seemed legitimate, especially since he gave faithfully to that ministry. After all, what could a church have to hide? I mean that sincerely. If this is a place that's doing God's work, why wouldn't you be willing to throw your books wide-open for everyone to see? These inquiries should be welcomed by church leaders. One would think that after looking at the finances, a person would see all the wonderful things being done to help people in need. As a result, anyone would be thankful to have given to an organization that's doing something great for God and mankind.

Unfortunately, financial openness is often not the case, which was proven true with my friend. Upon arrival, he was surprised to be met by not only the pastor and his wife, but also by a "tribal council" of sorts. As he entered the room, he looked around and saw an entourage of upwards of 20 people! This included other family members, the church secretary and her husband, a wealthy businessman and a professional athlete to boot!

I've tried hard to find any good reason for such a line-up. Here you have a guy who gave consistently, and I would say generously, to a ministry and all he wanted was to see where his money was going. Did he not have that right? Should he and his wife feel this kind of intimidation for just wanting to know? Shouldn't the church leaders appreciate such questions regarding the stewardship over God's finances? Shouldn't they realize that once their people saw how money was spent, they would be compelled to not only continue giving, but to give more?

Needless to say, the "books" given to my friend offered a vague display of the church finances, and without any detailed breakdown. They revealed nothing regarding salaries or specific expenses—just a veiled attempt at presenting something to satisfy the less inquisitive. After his visit with the "tribal council" that day, he wasn't voted off the island, but he willingly left. And who could blame him?

The lack of full disclosure regarding questionable financial decisions happens all the time. Most often people just leave. No one addresses the situation.

It is tragic.

There was an incident that occurred in our city that even shocked me. Below is a portion of the story initially written by Jeff Brumley for the *Florida Times-Union* and then updated on August 16, 2009, in the Sunday edition of Jacksonville.com.

Bethel Baptist Institutional Church is spending thousands defending itself from a lawsuit filed by three deacons who say they are worried about the way its leaders spend church money.

The problem, they say, is that the Revs. Rudolph McKissick Sr. and Jr. will not allow them and other congregation members to see how a $22 million loan has been used. Their suit to gain access to those records has been winding its way through Duval County Circuit Court for more than a year.

"We just want to see where the money went," one of the plaintiffs, William McCormick, said after a court hearing last month.

Whatever the suit's outcome, the Bethel case is a reminder of how lack of transparency - real or perceived - in church finance can generate everything from headaches to disgruntled parishioners to legal challenges.

But no matter who wins this or any other finance-related legal challenge or criminal case, experts say the fallout will land far beyond the sanctuary walls.

"Search the Internet and you'll find all too many stories of misuse of funds in churches, and when that happens everyone in the Christian world gets a black eye," said Dan Busby, president of Evangelical Council for Financial Accountability,

a Virginia-based ministry that seeks to bring church finances into the light of day.

The McCormicks and other Bethel leaders declined comment for this story, but, as Busby said, the Web is crawling with nightmarish church-money stories:

- In 1989, Jim Bakker was imprisoned after embezzling more than $150 million from his PTL cable network.

- Ellen F. Cooke, former treasurer of the Episcopal Church, admitted in 2006 to embezzling $1.5 million from the denomination.

- The Rev. Henry J. Lyons was ousted as president of the National Baptist Convention in 1999 and spent time behind bars for stealing $4 million from the denomination to help support a mistress and buy luxury homes and jewelry.

- Earlier this year, two Florida priests were sent to prison for stealing hundreds of thousands from a Catholic parish in Delray Beach.

These stories are sad but true, and they impact the public's view of the church. In this case, we have three men who are suing the church where they are deacons, just so they can see the financials.

How crazy is that?

Most people leave way before it gets to this point, and the abuse and insanity just continue. Although having a lawsuit involved is disturbing, seeing a few guys with the kahunas to put their foot down and say, "I want to see where God's money is going," is commendable.

I know I shouldn't be encouraging this kind of behavior. After all, what will outsiders think when members are suing the church? The reality is that the church has already lost the trust of many as a result of the rampant abuse and scandals. Maybe situations like this will help bring about some much-needed reform in the area of finances. What's more, it may give some people hope.

There are also those who say things like, "You shouldn't question the man of God," as if to say, "Go ahead and ask those kind of questions, but lightning may strike you at any moment."

I have even heard some go back to the Old Testament and say

that we need to be careful "not touch the Lord's anointed."[25] Actually, applying this verse here is such a terrible misuse of Scripture. It's absurd. Twisting Scriptures to mean that God's leaders shouldn't be questioned is basically manipulation. What's more, this can actually be classified as spiritual abuse in many cases.

So with all the nonsense that we see going on with churches and ministers, wouldn't opening the financials for all to see simply be wise? I do give credit to those churches that have their budgets and books wide-open. Furthermore, I applaud them. I would suggest giving your time and finances to these kind of churches.

If the books aren't open, or if you feel like you can't ask questions about the finances of the church, I would say that may be a strong indication that something is wrong. At the very least, certain individuals don't want you to see some things. The way some churches utilize funds may not be illegal or unethical; however, their use of finances may be considered wrong by those desiring to live like Jesus and belong to a church that emulates Him with their financial decisions.

A SACRED OFFERING?

Most of those who give to the church are giving an offering to God, a gift laid on the altar, so to speak, as in the Old Testament. Sometimes these are very sacrificial gifts from people who live very modestly or are on fixed incomes. I think its significance is often lost somewhere along the way as the money goes from the offering plate, to the back room to be counted, and then to the bank where it's deposited into the church's account. The whole process can eliminate the offering's sacredness, making it seem more like a financial transaction than a gift given unto God.

---

[25]The phrase, "Don't touch the Lord's anointed" is taken from 1 Samuel chapters 24 and 26. The problem is that people are using this to justify authoritarian leadership within the church with no regard for the actual context of David's statement. David is talking about whether or not he should do physical harm to the one who had been anointed as king. Comparing a pastor to the anointed king of God's people in the Old Testament is a pretty long stretch. Also, King David was later rebuked by the prophet Nathan for his sin of adultery and murder. David didn't respond by saying, "You shouldn't touch the Lord's anointed." Rather, he humbly received this rebuke and repented before the Lord. (2 Samuel 12:1-15).

When the finances of the church are seen as mere income or revenue, the use of these funds in ways that God never intended becomes easier to rationalize. In contrast, when these same finances are seen as sacrificial gifts given to proclaim the good news of Jesus and show the love of God to a broken world, attitudes are changed. A healthy understanding of this actuality should put the fear of God in those who handle His resources.

Pastors would then find their exorbitant salaries more difficult to receive. Some pastors in our city have salaries in the range of $200,000 to $300,000 a year from doing "the Lord's work." This amount doesn't include benefits and other perks that they receive. I know that I'm treading on thin ice with heated skates here, but that's OK. I truly believe Someone will be there to catch me, shall I fall through.

I have searched the New Testament and have come up empty trying to find something that would justify pastors receiving excessive salaries. Jesus and the leaders in the early Church emulated a life of total sacrifice. They realized that this world was not their home, and so they lived accordingly. I just can't imagine any of them living the kind of lifestyle that some of God's superstars live today. Well maybe Judas, but let's not go there.

Some people compare the salaries of pastors in large churches to the salaries of CEOs who run companies that bring in similar annual "revenue." On the surface, this way of thinking might sound logical and fair, but we're talking about two totally different entities. One actually exists to make money, while the other exists to glorify God. Also, we would do well to remember that when we're talking about making $100,000 or more, we're talking about a person going from being rich to filthy rich, especially in relation to the rest of the world.

According to the Global Rich List [26] a person who makes $100,000 is in the top 0.66% of the richest people in the world. Although there is some debate on how precise this tool is, most agree that those figures are fairly accurate. So, a salary of $100,000 would place someone in the top 1% of the richest people in the world! That means 99.34%

[26] www.globalrichlist.com

of the world lives on less than that individual. With that said, I don't know how you could describe this as anything but being rich.

The New Testament has a story where Jesus had an interaction with a very wealthy, young man. After He told him to sell everything he had and give to the poor, we read, "Jesus looked at him and said, 'How hard it is for the rich to enter the kingdom of God! Indeed, it is easier for a camel to go through the eye of a needle than for a rich man to enter the kingdom of God.' Those who heard this asked, 'Who then can be saved?' Jesus replied, 'What is impossible with men is possible with God.'"[27]

Basically, Jesus said that it takes nothing short of a miracle for a rich person to enter the Kingdom of God. Riches are often a hindrance to faith and can actually keep people from God. If this is the case, why would pastors desire to be rich?

One day I was having a conversation with a pastor of a fairly large church. He was at the point where his annual salary had reached more than $200,000. In the course of our conversation, he told me that he was pretty much set financially. The only thing left to do was to get the youth pastor and associate pastor to six figures. I don't think that was his main goal in life or anything like that, but that is what he told me. These statements would seem normal if I were talking to an executive or someone who owned their own business.

But a pastor?

Really?

In effect, his outlook was one of, "Now that I'm filthy rich, all that's left to do is to move the other guys into that top 1% of the wealthiest people in the world." Yeah, that sounds like something that would be right at the forefront of Jesus' thinking.

Consider the words of Paul when he wrote to Timothy, his young pastor friend, to warn him of those who would see the ministry as a means to financial gain:

"These are the things you are to teach and insist on. If anyone

---
[27] Luke 18:24-27.

teaches otherwise and does not agree to the sound instruction of our Lord Jesus Christ and to godly teaching, they are conceited and understand nothing. They have an unhealthy interest in controversies and quarrels about words that result in envy, strife, malicious talk, evil suspicions and constant friction between people of corrupt mind, who have been robbed of the truth and who think that godliness is a means to financial gain. But godliness with contentment is great gain. For we brought nothing into the world, and we can take nothing out of it. But if we have food and clothing, we will be content with that. Those who want to get rich fall into temptation and a trap and into many foolish and harmful desires that plunge people into ruin and destruction. For the love of money is a root of all kinds of evil. Some people, eager for money, have wandered from the faith and pierced themselves with many griefs" (1 Timothy 6:2-10).

Now I understand that God blesses some people with wealth. Nothing is inherently wrong with being wealthy. I get that. But I'm talking about ministers whose salaries are often paid by sacrificial offerings made to God by average people, many who have no hope of making that kind of money. Aren't we supposed to follow Jesus by the way we live and serve? Maybe it's me, but I just can't picture Jesus in a custom suit, staying at oceanfront resorts and eating at Ruth's Chris steakhouse regularly.

Call me crazy.

BREAKING "THE CODE"

So, what about the stuff in the Bible that talks about pastors being blessed?

"The elders (pastors) who direct the affairs of the church well are worthy of double honor, especially those whose work is preaching and teaching. For the Scripture says, 'Do not muzzle the ox while it is treading out the grain,' and 'The worker deserves his wages.' Do not entertain an accusation against an elder unless it is brought by two or three witnesses. Those who sin are to be rebuked publicly, so that the others may take warning" (1 Timothy 5:17-20).

What does "double honor" mean?

I would actually agree with those who have said that the phrase "double honor" could also be translated as "generous pay." I think those who shepherd the flock should be paid generously. They shouldn't have to worry about whether or not they can put food on the table and take care of their families.

The question is at what point do we cross over from being paid well to being overpaid? I know this is an ambiguous line that's hard to draw. However, based on the abuse that we have seen and the confidence that has been lost as a result, shouldn't we at least be willing to ask these questions? I'm not advocating across-the-board salary caps for pastors; I'm just pleading the case that we should live more like Jesus than like corporate America.

What if we took "double honor" to mean twice what the average person makes? Would that be enough? Let's say that the average income in an area is $40,000. Shouldn't a pastor be satisfied with making twice what the average person makes? Why would someone serving Jesus need more than that?

Paul says that we shouldn't even entertain an accusation against an elder unless it's brought by two are three witnesses. I would guess that I would have no trouble finding two or 3,000 who share my feelings. The problem is that the typical person would never raise such questions in fear of losing friends or being excommunicated.

Then the question is whether or not the salaries of pastors should be discussed publicly. I think Timothy's words in I Timothy 5:20 spoke to this point as well: "Those who sin are to be rebuked publicly, so that others may take warning."

I'm not saying that any pastor who makes over a certain amount is sinning. I will, though, unashamedly say that there are many whose lifestyles and handling of God's money is nothing short of sinful.

I now feel like someone who has broken "the code," so to speak. You know what I mean. There's an unwritten code that people on the inside just don't talk about certain things. Like, baseball players aren't supposed to rat-out the guy on steroids, and basketball players don't talk about teammates' marital indiscretions, or whatever. Pastors seem to have a similar code. For instance, I have heard a lot of people who openly express disdain for the televangelists who make millions, but not many people will openly talk about how much is too much of a salary for the average local church pastor.

Which brings me to another question. Why have we decided to start paying commissions to pastors? Whether we acknowledge it or not, that's basically what we do. If someone pastors a small church, he often gets paid a small salary. The bigger the church, the bigger the salary. It makes perfect sense, right? But where did that idea come from? Sounds like corporate America to me. "He runs a church of 2,000. Surely he should be paid $XXX,XXX." You fill in the blank with the ungodly amount.

Let's think this through. By paying a pastor based on the size of his church, we have created a very unhealthy system that may contribute to some of the problems we see within the church today. Let's say that I'm a pastor of a small but growing congregation, and I know that if the church grows, my salary will continue to grow. What is going to be my main goal? Growing the church. Isn't that supposed to be the goal anyhow? Not necessarily. In fact, I would actually say, "No. It's not supposed to be the goal."

The goal should be to honor God and to share His love with a broken world that desperately needs it. Jesus told the teachers of the law that the greatest commandment was to love the Lord your God with all your heart, soul, mind and strength and to love your neighbor as yourself.[28] Simply put, the goal should be to love God and to share that love with others. Now, I would say that when we carry out this commandment, the church will grow. Although the result may be the same, the way we get there is worlds apart.

If my goal is growth, then I will do whatever it takes—within reason—to grow. We've been programmed that numeric growth is equal

---

[28]Mark 12:30-31.

to success in the church world. This then leads to accolades and personal remuneration. So... show me the money!

And with the need for growth comes the need for bigger buildings. Come on. We all have seen *Field of Dreams*. Just build it, and they will come, right? Of course when we build bigger buildings, then we need to be sure the money is there to cover the enormous mortgage payment and utility bills. We may then be led to do things that we normally wouldn't do. We may even do some things that are just flat-out wrong, like paying more attention to the wealthy who walk through the doors and giving them preferential treatment. Regardless, we must be sure that our time is allocated to matters that will help growth. Not only does growth mean success and a bigger salary, it also is needed to feed the machine or monster that we have just created.

I recently had one of the most unbelievable conversations that I have ever had with a church leader. As we shared some of our personal stories and our mutual distaste for what I now call "institutionalized religion," my friend relayed one of the things that caused him to leave one of the most influential denominations among evangelicals. I just couldn't believe what I heard him tell me. Apparently the church where he was on staff wasn't growing fast enough for the powers-that-be, so he was given a special offer.

I kid you not—he said, "They offered me a baptism bonus. I was told that if I baptized a certain number of people, I would get a bonus check at the end of the year."

At first I thought he was joking and responded with my typical knee-jerk reaction of, "No way!"

He responded, "Yes, way. And that's not even the worst part."

"What could be worse than that?" I asked.

"Even though I didn't make it my goal, I actually ended-up baptizing more people than their goal, and guess what?" he asked.

"What?" I responded.

"They never even paid me the stinkin' money!"

Situations such as this should clearly demonstrate that we have drifted off track. Call me an idealist, but I just want to love Jesus, share that love with people, and train and equip others to do the same.

Right now, I serve in a role where I teach and lead a group of about 200 adults. I can honestly say that I'm more satisfied than I've ever been. I'm actually paid well, and I don't desire or need my salary to increase as we grow. Actually, I've found myself at times arguing with friends about my desire to reduce my salary. I know this sounds crazy to some, but the reality is that my family is taken care of, and I feel like we should function with some element of faith in our lives.

I think pointing out that our group is not made up of extremely wealthy individuals is important. The average income among those who attend would probably coincide with the average income in our city. And yet to this day, we have never had any money problems. Furthermore, we have never had to say "no" to any legitimate need that has been presented to us. God has always given us the ability to participate in helping those in need and giving to ministries that are doing great things for His Kingdom.

So what's the secret?

I wish there was one because then I could sell it and eliminate my salary from the church altogether. Nevertheless, we have discovered that it's as simple as listening and obeying the words of Jesus who said, "'Do not worry, saying, "What shall we eat? or "What shall we drink?" or "What shall we wear?" For the pagans run after all these things, and your heavenly Father knows that you need them. But seek first His kingdom and His righteousness, and all these things will be given to you as well'" (Matthew 6:31-32).

In other words, just seek God's Kingdom first in all that you do.

When it comes to making decisions, ask the question, "What's in the best interest of God's Kingdom, particularly when it comes to spending God's money?" Church leaders need to be willing to throw out conventional wisdom and the way church has always been done. Instead, they need to seek God's wisdom and His Kingdom when decisions need to be made.

As for buildings, seek first God's Kingdom, not your own. Buying land and constructing a facility may not always be the best solution. There are a lot of empty buildings these days. Church leaders need to be open to what God may want to give them. Also, schools, movie theaters, night clubs and other facilities can serve as good alternatives to traditional gathering places. And maybe something can be said for fasting, praying and waiting for God to work a miracle rather than depending on hired professionals to run your capital campaign.

I am reminded of a very sobering passage found in the Bible. In Luke 12:15, Jesus was approached by a man who asked Him to tell his brother to divide his inheritance with him. Jesus basically said, "Who has made me a judge between you?" He then said, "Watch out! Be on your guard against all kinds of greed; a man's life does not consist in the abundance of his possessions."

Then He told them this story:

"'The ground of a certain rich man produced a good crop. He thought to himself, "What shall I do? I have no place to store my crops." Then he said, "This is what I'll do. I will tear down my barns and build bigger ones, and there I will store all my grain and my goods. And I'll say to myself, 'You have plenty of good things laid up for many years. Take life easy; eat, drink and be merry.' But God said to him, "You fool! This very night your life will be demanded from you. Then who will get what you have prepared for yourself?" This is how it will be with anyone who stores up things for himself but is not rich toward God'" (Luke 12:16-21).

When "barns" get full, is building bigger ones always the best thing to do?

For some churches to spend upwards of $20 million on a building these days is nothing. Willow Creek Community Church in Illinois spent more than $73 million on their new state-of-the-art worship center in 2004. [29] That's a big ol' barn! Yet, that seems modest compared to the $123 million that First Baptist Church in Dallas has proposed to spend on their new campus.[30]

One hundred twenty-three million dollars. Really? For that kind of

[29]Wikipedia, "Willow Creek Community Church," Wikipedia, http://en.wikipedia.org/wiki/Willow_Creek_Community_Church, 03 March 2011.

[30]Prism Electric, "Historic Proportions: Prism Electric Tapped for Largest-ever Baptist Church Expansion," Prism Electric, http://www.prismelectric.com/news/?p=11, 03 March 2011.

cash, you might as well just build a giant rocket and your own space station somewhere. I just looked online and found that $100 million can get you your own 2,000-acre private island in the Caribbean. Or I guess you can just build a giant steeple and become the envy of many a pastors.

PERSPECTIVE

Some organizations claim that for $36, you can feed a child for a year. Others say that for $15 a month, you can provide medical care, clean drinking water and food for a child in need. Then the more widely known non-profits, such as World Vision, say that you can sponsor a child for about a dollar a day.

Based on World Vision's numbers, $20 million could support all of the needs of 5,479 children for 10 years! At $15 a month, $73 million would help 40,055 kids for an entire decade. And if you can feed a child for one year for only $36, then with $123 million, you could literally feed 189,814 children from the day they are born until they turn 18!

Think about it.

What does it mean to be rich

toward God?

"He who is kind to the poor lends to the LORD, and He will reward him for what he has done" (Proverbs 19:17).

Leaders need to be good stewards of the finances that have been entrusted to them. So when it comes to facilities, we should seek first God's Kingdom. When it comes to staffing and salaries, we should seek first God's Kingdom. We shouldn't just hire a particular position because that's what churches in the past have always done. And don't assume that every position must be full-time or even paid for that matter. If a position only requires 10 or 20 hours a week, then we should generously pay someone for those hours.

When you're thinking about spending money on things like marketing, be sure to put the Kingdom of God first in those decisions. When people are dying without clean drinking water and from other preventable diseases, does spending tens of thousands of dollars on marketing the church make sense?

Is that what's best for God's Kingdom?

What it comes down to is a basic question of faith. Do we believe that God's Word is true? If so, will we trust Him to do what He has said He would do in building His Church and providing all our needs?

He doesn't ask too much of us.

Just to seek first His Kingdom in all we do.

He promises to take care of the rest.

"Command those who are rich in this present world not to be arrogant nor to put their hope in wealth, which is so uncertain, but to put their hope in God, Who richly provides us with everything for our enjoyment. Command them to do good, to be rich in good deeds, and to be generous and willing to share. In this way they will lay up treasure for themselves as a firm foundation for the coming age, so that they may take hold of the life that is truly life" (1 Timothy 6:17-19).

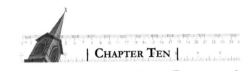

CHAPTER TEN

Confession is Good for the Soul

The confession of evil works is the first beginning of good works.
  ---St. Augustine

They say that confession is good for the soul, and I have found this to be true.

I'll never forget a particular night at the rescue mission. In one sense, it wasn't that different than any other time we had gone down there to serve. In fact, for everyone else, it was probably just like any other night. But for me, this night was very significant.

Typically, we would show up at the mission around six o' clock and hang out with the guys for a little bit before they did role call and went through the rules for the "newbies." After that, we had a short service, which included some music and an encouraging message. Someone from our group usually shared a part of their life with the hurting brothers and sisters. Stories of hope and encouragement would be told by real people dealing with real struggles who were finding strength in a present God.

On this night, it was my turn to share. Again, not much was different for anyone else, but for me, it was a night of confession. A time to come clean.

Often when you go to a place like a homeless shelter, you hear messages of hope and how their circumstances can change. They tend to focus on turning to God and trusting Him to provide for their needs and to help them get back on their feet, all of which are appropriate and helpful. However, this time my message would be a little different.

My intention was to encourage and challenge the men and women in the room. I wanted to encourage them to seek God for change and to believe that their life could be different. I also wanted to warn them.

PROSPERITY AND ENTITLEMENT

Somehow along the way, we have taken this beautiful message of God's love and forgiveness and equated it with pursuing the American Dream, as if the two coincide with each another. Follow God, and everything is going to be OK; you'll enjoy personal prosperity and happiness as you follow Jesus.

There are those who preach the message of prosperity in such a way that it comes off like, "Give God 10, and He will give you 20." Then you have those, like the "smiling pastor," who is always happy and never hesitates to tell you how God wants you to live a happy and pain-free life. There is also a much more subtle but equally dangerous message of blessing and prosperity that can easily lead to a sense of entitlement. This message is prevalent throughout the church in America today.

What has happened is that many spiritual leaders have modeled a life of "blessing" that looks a lot like the achievement of the American Dream. Therefore, those who follow Jesus begin to believe that if they live for God, they too can achieve the American Dream. What's more, not only can they have it, but they should have it. We then obligate God to provide it. We do "A," "B" and "C," and God is expected to give us "D." This way of thinking is a self-serving, formulaic faith and looks more like a mathematical equation than the mysterious Biblical Spirit-led relationship between God and man.

This type of "faith" relegates God to do our bidding. We do our part, and then God is duty-bound to do His part. In essence, we have changed the God of the Bible into a "god" who we have created in our own image. He serves us well and fits into our American culture and mindset.

Five years ago, if you would have accused me of preaching a prosperity gospel message, I would have vehemently disagreed with you. I would have pointed my finger at those guys on TV and said, "They're preaching a prosperity message; not me." I would have gone as far as to say that they were no different than the snake oil salesman of the past. I even regularly made fun of the whole "name it, claim it, buy it, frame it" message. I was nothing like that. Or was I?

Although I may not have been advocating this message of entitlement and prosperity with my words, I had been unknowingly sending out this message through my lifestyle. As I had alluded to in Chapter One, I had just bought a new car, nothing over the top like those "money-hungry preachers," but a $35,000 Acura TL. It was the nicest car I thought I could buy without raising too many eyebrows.

About the same time, my wife and I were looking to buy a new home. My dad, who was approaching 80 years old, was going to be moving in with us. With three kids of our own, we needed a little more space. I remember walking through the model home and saying, "This would literally be my dream house!" About a month later, we bought it. Again, nothing too extravagant but a very comfortable 3,000-square foot, $350,000 home.

I justified the costs of my house and car in so many ways. After all, we did a lot of entertaining, and we had many wealthy people who were a part of the church. Additionally, other staff members owned houses and cars that were much more expensive. But the bottom line was that we could afford it. I paid cash for the car and the mortgage was within our budget…kind of.

A year after we made these purchases, God started to open my eyes. I remember that the process had begun on a Wednesday evening after church. I had just finished preaching and was having a conversation with a couple in the parking lot. When we finished, I felt this strange sense of conviction and guilt. I didn't want them to see me getting into my car.

All I could think about was this beautiful family who lived very modestly and gave faithfully, and probably sacrificially, to the church. What would they think if they saw me getting into this new, flashy car?

They could think, "Wow, Pastor Vic is really blessed. If I live right and follow God, I could be blessed like that as well." Or they could think, "So that's where the money we gave to church is going." The thought of either was quite disturbing to me. I think I pretended to forget something in the building, and then after they left, I got in my car and drove home.

I don't know what it was, but something just felt wrong. I thought it through but couldn't come up with anything specific in the Bible that said it was a sin to own a nice car and a nice house. However, that didn't change what I was feeling. I kept thinking about my responsibility as a leader and how my lifestyle was an example to those around me. What was my life saying to people about what it meant to follow Jesus? "Follow God, and you can have all this, too?" I also had begun to think about the many people in our city and throughout the world who do all they can just to survive.

That was the beginning of my "holy crap" moment. About a week later, I sold the car, and as you have read, my life has changed quite a bit since then. I don't tell this story to say that people shouldn't own nice things or that anyone who has a nice car or a nice house needs to sell it or else they're sinning. I simply want to be honest and confess my own sin.

As much as I hate to admit it, my worldly possessions had started to become a part of my identity. Whereas owning such things might not be wrong, allowing them to define and own you is certainly wrong. And while we were in a position where we could "afford them," the reality was that if we lived differently, we could afford to help people who had needs far greater than what we could even imagine.

Before going through my "holy crap" moment, I believed my message was certainly more balanced than the prosperity message. I would say, "Jesus wants to be Lord of our lives. While this includes our finances, it's really not about money. God wants us to honor Him with our finances. In return, He promises to take care of our every need. He doesn't promise riches, but He will meet our needs." Pretty reasonable, right? The problem is that each of us has come to define our "needs" in light of our culture and what we see modeled before us.

What we deem to be our "needs" in America are often the things that many people in the rest of the world would never think of having, even in their wildest dreams.

I was hit with this reality a few years later when I took my first trip to Guatemala. We were celebrating with a family who had just received a new home through the "12x12 Love Project." They were so thankful that they were visibly overwhelmed by it all. I remember them thanking God and through their tears, thanking me, saying, "We never dreamed that we would ever own a home like this. Thank you so much, and thanks be to God!" I don't think there was a dry eye in the house.

I couldn't see the irony of the situation until afterward. There I was, standing with this family in a house that would be the equivalent of a small garage here in the United States. For them, this was a blessing from God beyond measure. They were overwhelmed with thankfulness that God would pour out His blessing on them in such a way. Then I thought, "How would I respond if my standard of living was reduced to that?"

How about you? How do you think you would respond?

I would guess that most of us would not be thanking God for such a blessing. Conversely, we would probably be crying out to God, asking why He had forsaken us and what we had done to deserve such poverty.

Think about this for a minute.

The same house.

The same God.

The same human beings created by Him and for Him. But yet two totally different responses.

One is filled with thankfulness and joy while the other feels forsaken, sad and possibly bitter. Why? Because we live in America. We have been trained to believe that we deserve what our culture and the church has put before us as the goal in life: the American Dream.

So as I stood before the men at the mission that night, I encouraged them to put their faith in Christ. I told them that Jesus came to this earth to give us life. He wants us to experience a fullness that far surpasses anything we can get from a bottle, pipe or pill. There is hope, and He does offer blessings to all who follow Him.

I also warned them to be careful and not fall into the trap that I had fallen into. I shared my story with them and confessed my sin. I showed them the tag I had cut off from the inside of my pin-striped, custom suit that the church had bought me. I had only worn it a couple of times, and on that night, I donated this suit to the mission. I now keep that piece of cloth tucked away in my Bible to remind me of a time when I began to find my identity in material things instead of in Christ.

The tag read, "Custom-Tailored for Vic Cuccia." I pleaded with them not to look for their identity in possessions but rather to find it in Christ alone. We were all created by God and for God. Each one of us was hand-crafted by Him. David put it this way: "For You created my inmost being; You knit me together in my mother's womb. I praise You because I am fearfully and wonderfully made; Your works are wonderful, I know that full well." [31]

He made us, and His works are wonderful. He has *great things in store* for us, but that doesn't mean that we should be people who *store up great things*. Our lives should be lived for the glory of God and His Kingdom, not to indulge our own selfish nature.

The reality is that life as we know it will one day be gone, and then what? What did we live for? What message did our lives speak to the world? What lasting effect will our lives leave?

I am reminded of something else that David once said:

"Surely everyone goes around like a mere phantom; in vain they rush about, heaping up wealth without knowing whose it will finally be. 'But now, Lord, what do I look for? My hope is in You.

---

[31] Psalm 139:13-14.

Save me from all my transgressions; do not make me the scorn of fools" (Psalm 39:6-8).

The American Dream is a lie.

That dream became my nightmare. It offers no lasting satisfaction. We call it a dream, and rightfully so, because that's what it is. It's not reality. Reality is that we are all created by God and have been put here on this earth to make a difference. Those who are just trying to survive and the thousands who die each day of preventable causes are, in a sense, casualties of the lie that many of us believe.

My hope is that the people of God will wake up from this dream and begin to understand the gravity of their decisions. The way we live has a ripple-effect that impacts the lives of countless individuals. As we chase the dream, there are others, including innocent children, who are living a nightmare.

Ironically, Jesus spoke so clearly about money and the deceptive nature of wealth; yet money continues to be the greatest area of struggle for many of His followers. Consider His commands in the following passage and take note of the exclamation points.

"Don't store up treasures on earth! Moths and rust can destroy them, and thieves can break in and steal them. Instead, store up your treasures in heaven, where moths and rust cannot destroy them, and thieves cannot break in and steal them. Your heart will always be where your treasure is. Your eyes are like a window for your body. When they are good, you have all the light you need. But when your eyes are bad, everything is dark. If the light inside you is dark, you surely are in the dark. You cannot be the slave of two masters! You will like one more than the other or be more loyal to one than the other. You cannot serve both God and money" (Matthew 6:19-24 CEV).

I have heard a lot people talk about the fact that we shouldn't store up treasures on this earth and that you cannot serve both God and money. However, I don't think I have heard many talk about what Jesus said between these statements. I mention this because it might be the key to understanding what He's trying to tell us here.

What we do with our money and how it affects us has a lot to do with how we view this world. Your eyes are like a window, and if you are seeing the world properly, you'll realize that the stuff of this world will all pass away. If you understand that only God's Word and His Kingdom will last, then you have all the light you need. If you can't see clearly, you'll find yourself in darkness. That darkness can easily lead you to be enslaved by material things and the almighty dollar.

According to Jesus, you cannot serve both God and money. You'll like one more than the other or find yourself more loyal to one than the other.

Where does your loyalty lie?

Who or what do you like more, God or money?

Does the answer you profess line up with the way you live?

What would the world be like if

everyone's priorities were the same as yours?

Think about it. Pray about it.

"If we confess our sins, He is faithful and just and will forgive us our sins and purify us from all unrighteousness" (1John 1:9).

Confession is good for the soul.

CHAPTER ELEVEN

Don't Stop Believin'

I believe in Christianity as I believe that the sun has risen: not only because I see it, but because by it, I see everything else.
  ---C.S. Lewis

I am still blown away when I think back to how God answered our prayer when we were in need of a gathering place for the church. Not only was it a confirmation to me that we were on the right track, it was also a reminder that God had not given up on His Church. In fact, with all the mess we see in the church in America today, God's grace remains. So He continues to use the church, flaws and all.

In no way am I suggesting that we overlook the issues that need to be challenged or changed within the church. That should be obvious by now. What I will suggest is that like God, we do not lose faith in the Church, this unstoppable force that exists to bring hope and healing to a broken world.

The church has failed in many ways, but its failures don't mean that the beauty and purity of the Church cannot be restored. For this to happen, some of us may need to humble ourselves and admit that we were wrong. Others may need to be willing to accept the apology and re-engage.

To be a follower of Jesus and to give up on the Church makes no sense to me. You can't give up on the Church because, whether you like it or not, you are the Church! It's not an institution or the place where we meet. The Church is and always has been the people of

God.

As we saw earlier in 1 Corinthians 12, Paul described the Church as a body made up of many parts. He went on to say that all the parts are equally important and necessary for the body to function properly.

This means you are important, and you can make a difference!

Although your contribution may feel like a single drop in the ocean at times, you have much to offer. Jesus chose 12 and changed the world. I believe He continues to call out to the highways and byways, seeking those who will answer the radical call to be His disciples.[32] When people begin to hear that call and respond, incredible things happen.

WHAT IF?

So let me ask you a couple of questions. What if we really began to believe the things we read in the Bible and actually put them into practice? What would life be like? I'm not exactly sure, because if I were to be honest, I would have to admit that I don't always live that way. I think living out what we read in the Bible would be a little more haphazard and risky than what most of us experience today.

The majority of our days are so routine and well-planned. Thank God for tools like Google Calendar and a million apps to help us plan and direct every part of our busy schedules. Then of course we have Facebook, which allows us to peek-in on what's happening with "friends" whom we haven't spoken with in 23 years. By the way, you know a problem exists when people's self-worth is attached to how many virtual friends they have or how many people "like" their latest status update.

I think someone should make a virtual hamster wheel app. Your Facebook profile pic could be superimposed on the head of a hamster while it runs endlessly on the wheel in its cage. Then pictures from your phone and Facebook could pop up on the screen while U2's "Running to Stand Still" plays in the background. I know that's a random thought, but maybe you get the point. Our days are so tightly

---

[32] If you are interested in knowing more about what it means to follow the radical call of Jesus, I would encourage you to read two books: "Radical" by David Platt and "The Pursuit of God" by A.W. Tozer.

scheduled, and then add in all the distractions. We end up feeling like we've accomplished a lot when we've actually done very little that really matters.

What if God wanted to interrupt your busy schedule once in a while?

Would He be able to do that? I think if we began to take the words of the Bible more seriously, our lives would have to change. For instance, what if we decided to believe that Jesus meant "Love your neighbor as yourself?" What would that look like?

If we took this command seriously, would we still walk by the elderly man's yard that's three weeks overgrown and mutter under our breath how awful it looks? Or, would we stop and do something about it? How about when your friend's car breaks down, and he doesn't have the cash to fix it, but you're sitting on a stack of money that you're saving for a rainy day? What about when you see a mom and her two children standing in the pouring rain at the bus stop? Or, when we are made aware of the horrors of things, like human trafficking and child slavery, which exist all around us?

I think that if we really believed the words of Jesus, we would be compelled to do something. Maybe we would give more of ourselves and our finances to others in need. We also might be willing to get our hands dirty and make time in our busy schedules for these kinds of "divine interruptions."

In fact, we're not taught to take the words of the Bible *that* seriously. If we were to be honest—even those of us who go to church regularly—we would have to admit this truth. We're taught certain verses to believe and even recite in order to get what we want or to feel better about ourselves. Then there are other passages that we soften up, pass over or write off as being culturally irrelevant today.

Is it only coincidence that many of the verses, which we deem irrelevant or not to be taken literally, are the ones that challenge us to live sacrificially or move us way outside of our comfort zone?

For instance, was Jesus really serious when he said that we should turn the other cheek? How about when He said that if anyone wanted to follow Him, they *must* first deny his or her self? What about when we are told to "love our enemies?" Or that we shouldn't chase after the things that the world chases after, but rather we should seek first God and His Kingdom, and then that which we need would be provided for us?

When Jesus told the story of the sheep and the goats, did He really mean that we were supposed to care for the sick, provide food and clothing for the poor, show hospitality to strangers and visit those in prison? Was He serious when He said what we do for the "least of these" (people), we in some way are doing them for Him? And will doing these kind of deeds be what characterizes those who'll be in heaven forever with Him, as told in the story?[33]

Maybe Jesus didn't realize the amount of responsibility we would have or how busy we would be today. Maybe He didn't know how corrupt the world would become and how dangerous it would be to do such things. Or maybe, just maybe, He simply meant what He said.

Have you ever had one of those meetings that you thought was just another lunch or dinner, and then it turned out to be a life-changing event? That happened to me when my friend Carl introduced me to Brock Johnson.

Carl had been telling me that I needed to meet this guy, but for whatever reason, it never seemed to work out. I thought our not being able to meet was because Brock didn't care too much for organized church, or pastors for that matter. He just said he was busy.

Anyhow, we finally did connect one day over a burger at Five Guys. As it turned out, we met only days before he and his wife and three children were moving to Guatemala.

We spent a few hours together that day, and he told me how his life had been radically transformed by Jesus. He shared with me how he went from being a successful executive for the Jacksonville Jaguars football franchise to feeling called to go and serve the poor in Guatemala. He had given up the fast life. He and his wife literally sold

---

[33] Matthew 25:31-46.

everything they had. Their belongings had been reduced to 10 plastic Rubbermaid bins that they were taking to Guatemala. Why would they do such a thing? Because they believed that Jesus told them to go.

Remember the story about the young rich man who came to Jesus? He asked Jesus what he must do to have eternal life. Jesus knew the man's heart and said, "You know the commandments," and then He rattled off a few.

The young guy responded, "I have kept all of those."

Jesus could have said, "Need I remind you that God hates pride?" But He didn't go there. Instead, Jesus dealt with the deeper issue, the issue of his heart. The man was rich, and apparently his stuff had a hold of his heart in a way that was coming between him and God.

This led to the following exchange:

"When Jesus heard this, He said to him, 'You still lack one thing. Sell everything you have and give to the poor, and you will have treasure in heaven. Then come, follow Me'" (Luke 18:22).

Jesus didn't say this to everyone who asked this question, nor did He make this a prerequisite for everyone that would follow Him. But He did for this man. The bottom line is that He wants our heart. If something else has it, then that must go in order for Jesus to be our Lord. What Jesus said to this young man some 2,000 years ago resonated with another young man 2,000 years later. As I said, if we were to really believe some of the things we read in the Bible, life can become a lot less predictable.

During my time with Brock, we exchanged stories and found that we had a lot in common. Both of our lives had taken a radical turn when we met Jesus. Although we both loved Jesus very much, neither of us was that excited about the Americanized-version of Christianity that we were seeing permeate the church. We wanted nothing more than to serve Jesus and try to be the Church that we see in the pages of the New Testament. We felt like we were swimming upstream against a strong current.

Our wrestling had led us on a similar journey but to two different destinations. Brock felt called to go to Guatemala and be the Church there, showing the love of Jesus to people living in desperate poverty. God told him to go, so out of obedience, he was going. No church or missions agency sent them; they had been called by the Spirit of God only. The plan was to trust Jesus and be led by the Holy Spirit as to what to do once they got there. There wasn't a whole lot of training or strategizing. Furthermore, they didn't even know a word of Spanish. Some would call this crazy; others would see it as an exciting step of faith.

I, on the other hand, felt called to stay here and try to be the Church in a culture where the poorest people would actually be considered rich in the mountains of Guatemala. I had plenty of training and had strategized with the best of them. My challenge was that I had begun to question it all. Planting a church is one thing; being the Church is another.

What if there was no plan to grow or become anything? What if that was left in God's hands? What if we simply tried to trust Jesus and be led by the Holy Spirit in how to serve and follow Him and help others do the same? Some would call that irresponsible or crazy; others would see it as a refreshing step of faith.

I left that meeting encouraged by the fact that some people still read the Bible and take what it says at face value. Some people still believe that God speaks today, and that all we need to do is listen and be led by His Spirit, regardless of how ridiculous that may seem to some.

I honestly didn't know if I would ever see Brock again. He would be getting on a plane and moving to Guatemala in just a few days. But I was genuinely excited for him and his family. I believed that God had great things in store for them.

A CRAZY IDEA

About a month later, I got an update from Carl on how things were going with the Johnsons in Guatemala. He shared with me some of their struggles as well as the amazing things that God was doing in their midst. Carl also told me that he found out that you could build a house for someone living in abject poverty for about $3,000.

Many of the people in this area live in one-room shacks made out of cornstalk and whatever else is available. Some use tarps as roofs and items like blankets, scraps of metal, and cardboard to cover parts of the walls to keep the cold winter winds from whipping through. Temperatures can get down into the 30s on some nights. Most of these homes have dirt floors that turn to mud during the rainy season. Often you'll find families of four or five people living in a structure like this with only one single mattress or just a makeshift pallet on which to sleep.

Carl and his wife Danae heard about the situation there and the conditions in which these people lived. They took it upon themselves to raise the money to build a house for one of these families. The only problem was, Carl had recently lost his job and really didn't have much to give.

He contemplated the strong words of Jesus calling us to love our neighbors as ourselves. He felt like God was telling him to sell his truck. Again, they didn't have much at the time. This truck was only worth a couple of thousand dollars, maybe, not to mention that he used this vehicle for any construction work he would get. Regardless, he couldn't shake the fact that he felt like God was saying, "Sell the truck."

Carl shared this with Danae, who responded as most loving, level-headed women would, by asking him if he had lost his mind! The discussion ended with her leaving the house. She eventually went to a coffee shop with her Bible. While thinking about what to read, she remembered that she and Carl had been talking about reading the book of Acts together.

Starting in the first chapter, it didn't take long before she got to Acts 2:44-45 "All the believers were together and had everything in common. Selling their possessions and goods, they gave to anyone as he had need." It was as if God Himself was speaking through the pages of Scripture.

She returned home and simply said, "OK. I think we should sell the truck." So they sold the truck and found themselves with about $500 left to raise.

When Carl told me about what they had done, I immediately thought we should get involved. By this time, we had about 75 people who were gathering on a weekly basis. Our goal was to love God and to love people, and in some way, join Him in bringing change to a broken world. So being a part of what God was doing in Guatemala made perfect sense. So we decided to get involved; after all, it was only $500.

I'll never forget the day when I was sitting in my mobile office (Panera Bread), sipping coffee in one of those big comfortable, cushioned chairs. I had begun my day as usual by checking my email. There I found a message from Brock. I opened it and began to read about the Mundo family. We had just given money to help build this family a home. As it turned out, the father was a pastor. He worked full time, and his wife and three children all worked as well. Together, they brought home what equaled about three dollars a day.

I had heard that more than a billion people in the world don't have clean drinking water and that more than two billion people live on less than three dollars a day. I had even preached about it. Still, it's one thing to hear statistics about poverty; it's another to put a name and a face to it. Ignoring poverty, pain and suffering is easy when you structure your life in such a way that you keep yourself isolated from them. But when you begin to see that poverty has a face and that these children are no different from your own, everything changes.

I looked at the pictures of this beautiful family that were sent with the story. The shack where they were living was deplorable, but there they stood with huge smiles. The construction had begun on their new home. The house was being made of block, and it was going to have a concrete floor and a metal roof. Trenches were being dug and rebar was being put in place. It was a beautiful site.

I sat in that comfortable chair thinking how I had just spent more money on a cup of coffee and a bagel than what this family collectively made in a day's wages. Tears filled my eyes. I thought about how this man was no different than me. We were both trying to serve and follow God. The only difference was that he was born in Guatemala, and I was born in America.

I then had this "crazy idea": "What if we stopped being so concerned about ourselves and decided to help those who were in need of basic shelter?" My next thought was, "What if we built one house a month for the next 12 months for people like the Mundo family who are living in utter poverty?"

To be honest, I didn't know if this was a thought of my own or God's Spirit nudging me to consider doing something crazy for Him and His Kingdom. Nevertheless, it was strong enough that I felt led to at least run the idea by the leaders of our faith community.

We got together for a meeting, and I shared with them the email that I received and what I was thinking. When I finished, I was surprised that every man in the room emphatically said, "I think that's God."

So the decision was made. We would build one house a month for the next 12 months and see what God would do. In addition, we decided to financially support the Johnsons on a monthly basis. We knew that as a result of our decisions, we would probably be uncomfortable for awhile.

To make a long story short, we had outgrown Andy's facility and were looking for a bigger place to rent. During our first year, we had grown to about 75 people, gathering together on Sundays and throughout the week in homes, etc. (For a group that wasn't focused on numerical growth, this was actually quite surprising.) On some Sundays, we would even have our little room full, and it was a bit tight.

We had previously determined that if needed, we had enough room in our budget to add about two to three thousand dollars to our monthly facilities expenses. In a real estate market that was pretty beaten-down, we thought that finding a place wouldn't be too difficult.

But every door seemed to slam shut. Our search for a new facility continued to come up empty.

So I can't tell you how excited I was at our decision to build the houses and support the Johnsons, even though any extra funds we had would most likely be depleted. Regardless, we knew it was the right thing to do.

We didn't plan on raising any money for the effort; we just figured we would spend what we had and then trust God for the rest. We made the announcement, and an immediate excitement swept through our little community of faith.

The response was amazing. We shared pictures and videos of the precious families we had begun to help, and people wanted to know how they could get involved. We simply let them know that $3,000 would build a house for a family in need, and to my surprise, money started pouring in. It was insane! People who I would never have expected to give that kind of money started coming up and saying, "This is awesome. We want to do a house."

A number of stories could be told, from the check that showed up from a college girl who was only a few months away from her wedding day, to the guy who was leaving church one Sunday and asked how many houses we had left to sponsor.

I said, "I think we have three left." (Actually, money started coming in faster than the houses could be built.)

He responded, "We got those."

"You got what?" I asked.

"We'll do those last three houses," he said.

I was floored. In less than 12 months, over $40,000 had been given to build these houses. Our goal was met without even trying.

It was all so crazy!

Another story involves the time when a guy visited my men's small group meeting one morning. After the group ended, he asked if we could talk. I said, "Sure," having no idea where the conversation would go.

He began by saying something like, "I've heard what you're doing in Guatemala. I have an idea of how to help, but I don't know what you're going to think about it."

I braced myself for what I thought might be the next get-rich-quick multilevel marketing scheme or something like that. I said, "Try me."

He then proceeded to tell me that he was a professional poker player and follower of Jesus. When he heard about our efforts in Guatemala, he felt like God was leading him to reach out to the poker community and get others involved. However, he didn't know if I would be OK with that because of the whole stigma surrounding gambling, etc. I told him that I thought God would be OK with poker players wanting to give money to help those in need and end poverty, so why wouldn't I be?

He then slid a check across the table with a sizable down payment for the house and said, "I should have the rest raised in about a month or so." And he did!

So this little group of Jesus followers, who would certainly seem insignificant in the land of mega-churches and million-dollar ministries, were being used by God to bring the love and hope of Jesus to families in Guatemala who were in desperate need. As a result, the "12x12 Love Project" was born, and the effort continues to this day.

In a little over two years, more than 40 houses were constructed. Families have not only received homes, but friendships have been built as well. Through the process, our desire is to show each family how much they are loved by both God and His people. We have built homes for some who are already followers of Jesus, like the Mundo family. We have seen others come to faith in the process. And then there are those we continue to pray for and show the love of Christ to, hoping that one day, they too will follow Him.

In addition to helping the families who have received houses, this effort has also impacted the local economy. All the materials are purchased from within the vicinity, which obviously helps neighborhood businesses prosper. Also each house is constructed by a crew of local men who work full time in this effort. In this area, having full time work on a consistent basis is rare. Our core construction team has now been employed full time for more than two years!

The "12x12 Love Project" has now become a non-profit organization that seeks to make a difference in the lives of those living in abject poverty in Guatemala, one house at a time. If you're interested in hearing the stories or getting involved, you can check it out by visiting its website at www.1212loveproject.org.

In the next chapter, you'll hear the other side of this story. I have asked Brock Johnson to share, in his own words, his perspective of

how a small group of Christ followers were used to make a big difference in another country.

CHAPTER TWELVE

When God Says, "Go!"

By Brock Johnson

God's work done in God's way will never lack God's supply.
---Hudson Taylor

My hesitancy to meet up with my buddy's "pastor friend" for lunch that day had nothing to do with a dislike of pastors (although to this day, Vic insists that it does!). Despite what he had heard about me, he couldn't have known that several of my best friends were current or former vocational pastors. Since then, a few more have joined my short list of closest friends, "IO 633 Cooch" included.

No, my hesitancy to meet Vic that day stemmed from a defensive position I had developed for Jesus and His Church. And from my own experiences up to that point in my life, most pastors—and Christians for that matter—did not share my stance. I had spoken to pastors and ministry workers. The majority of them were offended at my disdain for the lackadaisical routine of "doing church" and at my willingness to talk openly about it.

You should try something. With no resources other than your Bibles, begin a Bible study with a few close friends. (This is even more interesting if one or more of your friends are "theologian-types.") The point of the study is to determine what "Church" should look like. The hard part is to erase your lifetime of church experiences, preconceived notions, and Sunday morning memories. But try. Try to go into this study as if you had no prior church experiences or knowledge whatsoever.

If you're willing to do this, my bet is that you'll come away with something that looks nothing like the traditional American Sunday morning church.

Remember, many of my closest friends are pastors of American churches. I praise God that many are doing things differently and are honestly using the Scriptures as their roadmap. But I do believe that the philosophy to avoid the church planting/growing techniques modeled after western strategies of business success, and instead, use God's word alone as the guide is the exception, not the norm.

God did a revelation in my heart through a study such as this. The only difference was that we didn't set out to "do" the study; it just happened. As we studied the gospels, followed by the book of Acts, the power of God's Word was transforming. The empty motions of religion were unmasked, and the true calling of the Church of Jesus was revealed. For me, I began to understand how little I knew, and how God's call to being a Christian was unlike everything else I had ever heard.

I enjoyed my lunch with Vic Cuccia. I appreciated his journey that had gotten him where he was. Still standing after some dirty religious street fights, he seemed to remain committed to his calling as a pastor, passionate about Jesus, and devoted to doing something about it. He shared some hesitations about jumping back into "organized church in America." But he believed God was doing something different within the small community that he was being called to lead.

Three days later, I arrived in Guatemala with my family. Unaffiliated with any organized church or mission agency, we believed God called our family to this impoverished third-world country to help some of the poorest of the poor.

Our first few months on the ground were tough on the family. We didn't know our way around, nor did we speak a word of Spanish.

Just going to buy some groceries or run a simple errand was enough to bring on a serious headache. While we never doubted our calling to Guatemala, after a couple of months, our prayers started sounding something like, "Uhhh, what now, God?"

I heard from Vic again during this time of seeking and struggling. I'll never forget his email. He explained how they had outgrown their current gathering site and had begun saving money to find something bigger. They had been praying and saving in order to find an adequate place to gather when God intervened.

A couple weeks earlier, Vic had read the story I sent him about the first family for whom we had ever built a home. Pictures of this family filled him with compassion for those living in poverty. His heart broke as he considered their needs versus those of his church community. And thus came the "crazy idea" he mentioned in the previous chapter.

Instead of expanding into a much-needed larger meeting space, Vic felt led to give the money away to people who were physically suffering. Supported unanimously by the leadership team of Journey Church, the "12x12 Love Project" was born. Twelve houses were built in 12 months for families living in extreme poverty.

God perfectly initiated the "12x12 Love Project" to accomplish several things. I would be naïve to suggest that I can see or know even a fraction of a percent of His purposes, but thankfully He made a few of them obvious to us.

First, the timing was a needed encouragement and confirmation for my family. While we were taking steps of obedience into unknown territory, and genuinely struggling to get by in a third-world country, a pastor of a small church in Florida was struggling to accept anything that resembled going through the motions. While the "standard procedure" of where they were as a church suggested saving money for a larger gathering space, the procedure of the Holy Spirit was leading a completely different direction.

I was sitting in a Guatemalan internet café the day I received Vic's email. I vividly remember being unable to control the emotion that overwhelmed me. After each sentence or two I was sucking up tears, looking upward, and saying the most genuine "Thank you's" I had said in a long time. God was shedding some light into the darkness where He had called us. He was laying out our next steps. And He was giving us confirmation that we were exactly where He had called us to be.

Meanwhile, God was starting an awakening within a small church body in Jacksonville, Florida. From talking with Vic, I realized that the excitement was evidently inspiring their faith community and giving them hope. The wave of support, radical giving, mission trips, prayers and encouragement that would follow was beyond explanation. Seemingly overnight, people who we had never met became like family to us. The stories and images from the impoverished villages in Guatemala captured their hearts. Amidst what was being called an American economical crisis, the support that came in from this small church was incredible.

The following is a portion from my email response to Vic:

...When we left for Guatemala, we had no funds raised, no sending organization, no official "mission," and no agenda or even basic plans. God just said, "Go." We respectfully declined all "rational" advice from both Christians and non-Christians. Not because it was bad advice, but because God had spoken loudly and clearly. Your email below led me to the hardest cry I have enjoyed in a very long time. I heard God's voice as I read your email, saying, "I've had these plans for you all along. This is just the beginning. Isn't following Me a thrill?"

Journey Church...supporting the activity of the Holy Spirit in a 3rd-world country...through a family who is not a "member" of their church...and in fact a family they have never even met! How beautiful. Only Jesus works this way. I cannot tell you how much this excites me...

During the 2 ½ years following that email, over 50 homes were donated to Guatemalan families in need. God's hand of blessing over this ministry has spoken for itself as hundreds of lives have been changed. Journey Church has sent numerous short-term missionary teams to Guatemala to serve, and others are preparing to join us here full time. And it's just the beginning. Additional ministries have begun. God is casting a larger vision for the ministries here as we seek deeper, long-term change for the local communities.

As I think about the connection between my family and Journey Church, I'm drawn to the similar approach towards church, life and ministry. There is a strong shared belief that real ministry is carried out in the daily seeking and following of Jesus. God's Word is enough, and we should read it, take it literally, and follow it. The current of American culture is gradually leading us further and further from Biblical culture.

The reality is that the Biblical Dream and the American Dream are in direct conflict with one another. While one teaches to give your life away for God and others, the other encourages to build and to store for your own sake. The American Dream says, "Go out there and get all you can. Make as much money as possible. Make the best life possible for you and your family. Save and be wise with your money so that you can enjoy your future and your retirement."

The American Dream could be defined as the accomplishment of success, fame and wealth through hard work. It sounds good. It's generally received as admirable, respectable, and upright. But putting aside all bias and all American patriotism, are you willing to consider the ideology of the American Dream in light of the teachings of Jesus? Do you see how incorrect, Biblically speaking, the rigid pursuit of success, performance and happiness really is?

What Jesus taught is more like "the pursuit of fulfillment through dying to yourself, sacrificing for others, and suffering for Christ's sake."

Maybe this is the appropriate time for the qualifier that notes how thankful I am to be an American citizen. Without a doubt, that is true. I'm thankful for my American freedoms, and I'm thankful to those who fought for them on my behalf. But as I grow in my faith and surrender completely to the teachings of Jesus, I am forced to take more seriously the contradictions between His teachings and the many achievement-centered values that I grew up around. My desire for Christians in America is to embrace the many freedoms and opportunities we have and use them to become more radically selfless—helping others all over the world who don't have the same good fortune.

Usually when Jesus spoke of true faith and eternal life, He did so by describing the cost for following Him. It was never made to sound easy, sugar-coated, or even desired. In fact, the Biblical Dream was typically approached more like a warning than a warm invitation.

"Whoever wants to be My disciple must deny themselves and take up their cross daily and follow Me. For whoever wants to save their life will lose it, but whoever loses their life for Me will save it" (Luke 9:23-24).

"If the world hates you, keep in mind that it hated Me first. If you belonged to the world, it would love you as its own. As it is, you do not belong to the world, but I have chosen you out of the world. That is why the world hates you...If they persecuted Me, they will persecute you also" (John 15:18-21).

These are not isolated passages being cut and pasted to make a point. This is the common theme throughout Jesus' message. Following His death, resurrection, and the coming of the Holy Spirit, the theme continued with the disciples and into the early Church.

So, if I can dare ask...how can we reconcile these teachings to the manner by which we live out our faith on a daily basis? How can we justify any type of religious routine? How can we settle for going through motions that lack sacrifice, faith, risk and even danger? Don't they seem like the minimum that Jesus asks from us?

Somewhere along the way, particularly in our wealthy, western culture, we decided to make Christianity convenient and comfortable. We decided to re-define "church" to be a place we go or an activity in which we participate. Think about how often we use the phrase "going to church." Can you imagine asking Jesus or any of His disciples, "Where do you go to church?" or "What time does church start?"

I'm pretty certain they would look at you like you were crazy. Those questions would make absolutely no sense. The calling to be a member of the body of Christ, the Church, is something to which you give your entire life. The disciples lived and breathed it. Their belonging to the Church led them to foreign lands and empowered them to heal, preach and cast out demons. It stretched them beyond their capabilities, brought them under heavy persecution, and ultimately led them to their death.

"Hey Luke, what are you doing after church?" When you really think about it, a question like that is hilarious. Maybe disgraceful is a better word. Although it may seem like semantics, what we are implying is that "church" begins and ends. How sad that we have lowered what it means to be a member of the all-powerful, all-transformational Church of Jesus Christ to such frivolous standards.

At this point, you may be asking, "So where is the life, hope and joy that we are supposed to find in Christ if we're all called to sacrifice, persecution and suffering?" While it defies logical and practical thinking, it's in there…

CESAR

Cesar is a friend of mine who lives in a shack in the middle of a beautiful Guatemalan forest. He is a husband and a father. When he was 26, he was enjoying a normal life. Cesar had a beautiful wife and was starting a family. He had a pretty good job (any job in rural Guatemala is a good job), and he was a star in the local men's soccer league.

Suddenly, his back began to bother him. For three years, he continued working his manual labor job, but with each year, the back pain grew worse. Soon, he couldn't bear the pain to even get out of bed. With limited resources, Cesar and his family began to seek medical help. What they discovered was terrifying. Cesar had an incurable and fatal degenerative bone disease. He was told he would not live much longer and that he would be bedridden for his final months or years.

By this time, Cesar had three beautiful young children. As Christians, Cesar and his wife believed God for healing. But they also began to accept the reality that God's will for their life may be drastically different than anything they had ever imagined.

After enduring three years of deterioration, the pain and suffering grew to its worst. In the most excruciating night of pain that Cesar can remember, he was surrounded by doctors and family. His doctors advised him that he would not make it through the night. A wife prepared herself for life without her husband, and young children prepared to say goodbye to their daddy.

Cesar slipped into a coma. He recalls the story beautifully. "I looked down and saw angels at my feet, their beauty indescribable. Each one took the weight of one of my legs in their arms and gently caressed them. As they comforted me, a distinct voice whispered into my ear. The voice was very clear and very close. When I turned to look for the person, no one was there. But three times the voice said the same thing: "Read Matthew 9:12."

After three months, Cesar awoke from the coma. That was several years ago. Today, if you have the privilege to visit Cesar, you will leave his home blessed beyond measure. He has the majority of God's Word memorized. He preaches God's power, grace, mercy, love and mystery better than any trained evangelist I have ever heard. Weighing next-to-nothing and fighting through severe head, jaw, throat, back and leg pain, he shouts worship songs to his Heavenly Father with heartfelt depth and passion. He looks you in the eye, asks you questions, listens intently, and longs to know you.

It's hard to explain, but I always come away from hanging out with Cesar feeling deeply loved. Yes, I am always challenged, convicted and awed at his committed life of steadfast faith. Everyone who meets him is. But as I walk home from his house—every single time—I come away with an overwhelming confidence in the fact that he loves me and cares for me. Without a shadow of a doubt, I know that he prays for me, for my wife and for my kids. I cherish those prayers because I know that God hears the prayers of a righteous man. [34]

My point goes much deeper than sharing a heartwarming story about a sweet Guatemalan family. The point is that I have never seen a greater expression of life, hope and joy than I have through the life of a man who happens to be suffering through a long, painful, terminal disease. It simply defies logic. It destroys the false teachings of the prosperity gospel, extinguishing its flames with the refreshing Living

---

[34]James 5:16.

Water of Jesus.

Today, a new home is being built for Cesar's family through the "12x12 Love Project." This one is unique, being constructed throughout with wheelchair accessible sidewalks and with lots of windows so he can see the beautiful Guatemalan forest and wildlife from his bed. While Cesar is very thankful for his family's new home, he always reminds us that his real home is not here.

"In my eternal home," Cesar said, "I will run on streets of gold with a new and perfect body. I will be in the presence of my loving Heavenly Father. I will run, jump, and play soccer again. But until then, I will give thanks to God for the life that He has given me, for my family, and for my sickness. I ask Him every day to glorify Himself through my weakness."

Cesar's testimony reminds us that true victory is not found in this life and its temporary gains. It's not found in comfort, security or even in friends and family. It's not found in a career, salary, home, education, vacations or retirement. Rather, it is found in making the name of Jesus famous, and this is done as we give ourselves away completely for His sake.

As a husband and father of three children who are currently 14, 12 and 9 years old, I think about this cost on a regular basis. We live in one of the most dangerous countries in the world. Already known for kidnappings and ranked 4th in the worldwide murder rate, we are also becoming one of the gang and drug cartel capitals of the world. Just last week I saw a special on Fox News titled "Guatemala: America's Third War." The story detailed the mass departure of Mexican drug cartels to Guatemala, suggesting that the ramifications for Guatemala will be completely unmanageable.

Periodically, my wife and I are tempted to change course and let safer, more practical thinking prevail. There was the time when the father of my daughter's classmate was kidnapped. This was followed by another kidnapping of an employee at my children's school. More recently, one of my daughter's friends left their school because her brother was killed in a gang/drug-related shooting. One day, she just wasn't there, and eventually we were told that her family had quietly moved. Just last week while we led a group of American missionaries into a remote village, my life was threatened as a group of intoxicated men yelled, "Kill Brock Johnson," followed by gunshots from one of their 9mm handguns.

I'm not claiming to be suffering. I've never been tortured or beaten for sharing the gospel. But I'm saying there are moments, moments when my heart skips a beat because I can't locate one of my kids in a public place. Or, when my wife is late from running an errand and is not answering her phone. Or, when the police who are known for their overt corruption and connections to the kidnapping rings, pulled over our car for no reason.

As I write, I am watching my young son sleep next to me. His two older sisters are sound asleep in the next room. Sometimes I look at them and ask myself, "Why am I doing this? Why do we live here?" Not only are there the physical safety risks, but what about their education? We had such a sweet gig back in suburban north Florida.

Psalm 127 says that our children are like arrows in the hand of a warrior. If nothing else, I believe my calling as a parent is to sharpen the three arrows that God has entrusted to me. They are not mine; they are His. He did not give them to me to simply teach how to get ahead in this life and pursue fame and success as the general worldview suggests. He gave them to me for one reason: to sharpen them as arrows, preparing them to be used as His weapons in the most critical battle ever fought.

We all exist for the same purpose—to glorify God and to make Jesus known to all people. Anything less is empty and temporal. We are all arrows for God to draw back in His righteous bow, bringing glory to Himself as only He can do. Amazingly and mysteriously, He allows us to choose whether or not we will enlist ourselves for battle.

But enlisting means more than attending church and saying nighttime prayers. It means more than raising your hand to "believe" while every eye is closed and every head is bowed. Instead, enlisting is more like raising your hand and giving your life to questions like these: *Who is willing to follow Me anywhere? Who will give Me everything, all of your time, your health, your gifts, your money, your energy and your passions? Will you trust*

Me to step into the dark and unknown? Will you abandon your comforts for Me? Will you believe My promises? Am I worth that to you?

Maybe the biggest lesson I'm learning in the foreign mission field is that there are no "right" methods, programs or procedures. There is only surrender. If we are willing to surrender ourselves fully, allowing God to have everything we have, only then will we learn about His methods. For some, this calling could mean becoming a missionary to the corporate world, medical field, or construction job site. For others like Vic, it's pastoring a local church in America. And yet for many, it means going out to all the nations to make Him known.

Whatever the case, it is the responsibility of all of us—as Christians—to not let the greatest and most critical story ever told get watered-down to the level of "somewhere to go on Sunday morning."

I am thankful to be partnered with Vic Cuccia and Journey Church as we strive to reclaim God's purpose for His Church. Will you join us in this fight? Let's read our Bibles anew from a fresh perspective… and be filled with the faith that moves mountains (Matthew 17), stops the sun (Joshua 10), parts the sea (Exodus 14), heals the sick (Mark 16) and raises the dead (Matthew 10). Let's be willing to give ourselves away for the One that did the same for us (Romans 5). Let's fight for the cause of the real Church of the Holy Spirit (book of Acts), and not settle for anything less.

Chapter Thirteen

You Can Dooooo It!

I am a little pencil in the hand of a writing God who is sending a love letter to the world.

---Mother Teresa

Have you ever wondered if you could make a difference in the world? I have. There have been moments when I've questioned whether or not I had anything at all to offer. That was before I realized that, throughout history, God has used ordinary people to do some amazing things.

A chapter in the Bible that I really like is Hebrews 11. Some people have called this chapter "God's Hall of Faith." It begins by describing what faith really is: "Now faith is being sure of what we hope for and certain of what we do not see. This is what the ancients were commended for" (Hebrews 11:1-2). The chapter then goes on to tell the stories of some of the great men and women in Biblical history.

The writer reminds us that it was by faith that Noah built the ark. It was by faith that Abraham, when he was called by God to go, just went, even before he was given the destination. Moses and the people passed through the Red Sea by faith. And it was by faith that Rahab the prostitute welcomed and hid the Israelite spies that Joshua had sent to check out Jericho.

Each of those mentioned did some great things for God, and they were commended for their faith. It was their faith that caused them to live differently and to trust God. As we continue reading in Hebrews 11, we are told their faith centered on the reality that ultimately, this world was not their home.

"All these people were still living by faith when they died. They did not receive the things promised; they only saw them and welcomed them from a distance, admitting that they were foreigners and strangers on earth. People who say such things show that they are looking for a country of their own. If they had been thinking of the country they had left, they would have had opportunity to return. Instead, they were longing for a better country—a heavenly one. Therefore God is not ashamed to be called their God, for He has prepared a city for them" (Hebrews 11:13-16).

Each of these people had an understanding that what is experienced here on earth is not the end game. There is something more. As a result, they were *sure of what they hoped for and certain of what they did not see*, and so they lived accordingly.

What about you?

What are you living for?

The last time I checked, the mortality rate is still hovering right around 100%. The reality is that you and I are going to die.

Then what?

Will any of what we have invested our lives in really matter?

What if we chose to believe, like those that have gone before us, that this world is really not our home and that God is preparing a place for us? What if we believed that while we're waiting to join Him, there are things He would have us do that would show His love to a world that desperately needs to see it?

This is where I used to get stuck. I was plagued by questions like, "What could I have to offer God?" and "How could I make any difference in this world?" Then I realized something. Throughout history, God has been in the business of using average, everyday people, some of whom were even more messed-up than me. Remember the list of people above: Noah, Abraham, Moses and Rahab? Each of them had their own issues.

After the ark finally landed on dry ground, do you know what Noah did? He got drunk and passed out buck naked;[35] Abraham was a liar. Out of fear, he gave his wife to another man, saying that she was his sister;[36] Moses was a murderer before God even chose him to lead His people;[37] and as for Rahab, well her name says it all—"Rahab the prostitute."[38]

These people all had their own issues, yet they were all commended for their faith and were used by God to do great things. I think that God reveals their flaws to us for a reason. It's His way of saying, "It doesn't matter how messed-up you are. I have created you, and there are things on this earth that you are to do." He's like Rob Schneider's character in the Adam Sandler movies, cheering us on, saying, "You can dooooooo it!" Ok, maybe he's not like Rob Schneider, but you know what I mean.

God uses ordinary people to do extraordinary things. He even uses messed-up, dysfunctional people like me. So what's your excuse? Whatever it is, it's not good enough. You were created by God and for God, and there are things in this world that He has for you to do.

I often say, "The world should be a better place because you're alive." I really believe that. We were all created by God for a reason.[39] It's up to us to choose to follow Him and be a part of His plan. When you do, you begin to fulfill your part in making this world a better place.

I believe that much of the pain we experience in the world is the result of individuals who have missed God's purposes for their lives.

This morning, I read in the paper about a guy who was sentenced to life in prison for human trafficking. He had held a young girl captive in a hotel here in Jacksonville and sold her to men who would pay $20 for a 30-minute session with her.

I think most of us would agree that this guy is sick and deserves the full extent of his punishment...and then some. But I have to ask a

---

[35] Genesis 9.
[36] Genesis 20.
[37] Exodus 2.
[38] Joshua 2.
[39] Ephesians 2:8-10 and Colossians 1:15-17.

question: Do you think that God created this man to do these things? Was this the reason God put him on this earth?

No way!

I believe that God created him to reflect His glory, and there are things that God desired for him. He made a choice to turn away from God, and in doing so, he missed the purposes of God for his life. He has continued down that path, making similar choices that have resulted in horrific pain being inflicted upon an innocent, little girl.

There are a lot of people who believe that everything that occurs is God's will or desire. I don't believe this for a minute. I don't believe that it was God's will that this girl was kidnapped and treated like a piece of meat to be sold to perverted men. I would say that the pain she suffered was not a part of God's plan but was actually the result of numerous people choosing sin over God's perfect will for their lives.

God allows such things to happen, but He didn't plan them, and He certainly didn't initiate them. In 1 Timothy 2:1-6, we're told that God's will or desire is for all people to come to know the truth and be saved from sin and its devastating consequences. Although that doesn't always happen, it is His will or desire.

The world should be a better place

because you are alive.

This life does have meaning. You were put on this earth for a reason. Do you have any clue as to what that is? Have you ever slowed down long enough to take a deep breath and ask God why you're here?

CHOICES

I truly had no clue what God would do through that "crazy idea" I had. Now I can look back and trace the hand of God and see things I could never have dreamed. If God could use someone like me as a part of His plan to accomplish some measure of good in this world, I assure you that He can use anybody.

I don't come from a long line of pastors. In fact, I only went to church a handful of times when I was growing up. By age 21, I was an alcoholic and was smoking weed everyday—morning, noon and night. I was a mess. You would think I would have come to my senses after losing a brother to cocaine, but even that wasn't enough to wake me up. But God by His grace reached through this mess-of-a-life and saved me from myself. He revealed Himself to me, and I chose to follow Him.

Life is about choices. Will you choose to believe?

My friend Carl chose to sell his truck to help raise the money to build that first house. He believed that God was leading him to do that, and he simply wanted to be obedient. Not only did God use Carl's act of obedience as a catalyst for the "12x12 Love Project," but within a matter of weeks, Carl got a new job and a new truck. His boss gave him a much nicer truck than the one he had and told him to just pay him whatever he could, whenever he could, and not to worry about it.

I'm not saying, "Do this for God, and He will do that for you." What I am saying is that there is nothing better than following as God leads. And sometimes when God asks you to give up something, it's only because He has something better in store for you. That "something better" isn't always a monetary blessing, but sometimes it is.

During the course of that first year, we built 14 houses and showed the love of God in a tangible way to 14 families who were in desperate need. As blown-away as I was over the response of people who gave, nothing could have prepared me for what was to come.

It began with a phone call from a friend who was a part of Journey. He said he needed to talk to me and asked if we could go to lunch. I'll admit I was almost certain that the reason he wanted to get together was to tell me that he and his wife were going to be leaving our church.

I guess my own insecurities were mixed with the fact that we were not this refined group of people with a slick Sunday morning presentation. Journey is a motley crew of sorts. We might not appear all that different on the surface to a first-time visitor, but the heartbeat is quite different than many churches today.

We purposefully don't structure our services or ministry to appeal to consumer-minded Christians. We gather on Sundays to worship together through song, and then we teach from God's Word. Both are used for the expressed purpose of preparing us for what we feel is most important—to live the other six days for Christ and His Kingdom. Also, I regularly remind people that there are a lot of great churches in our city and that we realize Journey isn't for everyone.

All of this played into my thinking. I figured that my friend was going to let me know that the church just wasn't a fit for them. I have heard it before: "There are some things that we really like about the church, but we're looking for this, that and the other for our family."

My usual response to statements like these are, "There are a lot of places in Jacksonville where you can find that, so I will pray that God leads you to whatever is the best fit for you and your family."

The shock came when we sat down. One of the first things that came out of his mouth was, "I'm not the kind of guy who says that I hear God speak to me that often, but there is something that I've been feeling and I needed to talk to you about it. I think God is telling me to help us get a new building."

He continued to share how he couldn't shake the thought and how he felt it was God leading him. He then told me about a business deal that he had brewing. "If this happens, and I am pretty sure it will, I am prepared to give $55,000 toward a new building." I was speechless.

This began a string of events that could have only been orchestrated by God. About a week later, we received a check in the mail for $10,000 from a family who had only visited a handful of times. Included was a note that said, "Use this for the new building." The timing of this was uncanny, particularly because we hadn't spent much time talking about needing a new building. There was no fundraising campaign or pleas for money.

About this same time, I received a phone call from a realtor. He had my name from a year earlier when we had actually been looking for a building. He said, "Hey, are you guys still looking for a place for your church to meet?"

I responded, "We haven't really been looking, but based on some current events, we probably need to be."

"Well I may have your place," he said. He then went on to tell me about a space that was currently being used as a night club and was in the eviction process.

We were open to anything, so we went and checked it out. Although it smelled like stale beer and had the most awful mauve carpet throughout, it was actually pretty cool. It had a huge bar, a bunch of disco lights and a giant stage. It seemed like our kind of place. So we asked him to forward us the numbers, and we began to pray.

I was sitting in Panera Bread (where God likes to meet me) when I received the details on the building. While I was in the midst of forwarding the information onto the members of our leadership team, I received an email from my friend who had committed the $55,000. The subject stated, "Call me asap."

I picked up my cell phone and gave him a call. He told me that he had been talking about our ministry to his business partner and that he wanted him to meet me. We set up lunch for the next day.

I brought Chris Steed to the meeting because at that time, he helped oversee missions and benevolence at Journey. After being introduced, we began to share the things that God was doing through our community of Christ followers. We discussed Guatemala and what we were involved in there. We also talked about the ways in which we were showing the love of Jesus to those within our own city.

My friend interrupted about this time and said, "I think it's funny that I've been telling him about how we need a new building, and all you're talking about is Guatemala and helping people. You're not a good salesman." That may have been one of the best compliments I had received in a long time.

The real shock came when his business partner looked at us and said, "I just really appreciate that you guys are real, and that you're not here trying to sell me on anything. I think what you're doing is great, and I want to be a part of it. I'm going to write you a check right now for $25,000."

You could have picked up my chin from off the floor.

This was a man who I had never met and who had never visited one of our Sunday morning gatherings. As a matter of fact, I understood that he didn't regularly attend church anywhere. Yet he apparently had a heart for God and was moved to be a part of what we were doing.

In a three-week period, we basically had a new building find us, and we received $85,000 to pay for the new facility's renovation. This doesn't include $20,000 that was donated earlier by a young, single guy in our church. So in total, we had more than $100,000 to put toward a new building, all of which came in totally unsolicited.

It was almost as if God was saying, "Do things My way, and I'll take care of your needs." Oh wait. He did say that!

"'And why do you worry about clothes? See how the flowers of the field grow. They do not labor or spin. Yet I tell you that not even Solomon in all his splendor was dressed like one of these. If that is how God clothes the grass of the field, which is here today and tomorrow is thrown into the fire, will He not much more clothe you—you of little faith? So do not worry, saying, "What shall we eat?" or "What shall we drink?"' or "What shall we wear?" For the pagans run after all these things, and your heavenly Father knows that you need them. But seek first His Kingdom and His righteousness, and all these things will be given to you as well. Therefore do not worry about tomorrow, for tomorrow will worry about itself. Each day has enough trouble of its own'" (Matthew 6:28-34).

When all was said and done, we signed a three-year lease on the space and were able to renovate it to meet all of our needs. All of this occurred without me or anyone else having to get up and twist people's arms for money. Furthermore, we never took a single offering for the facility.

Isn't it funny how we find ourselves in shock when God simply does what He says He'll do in the Bible? For us, this was the second time we experienced something like this. The first came when the group had outgrown our house, and we met Andy, the man who had the dream. Now after outgrowing that space and showing love to our "neighbors" in Guatemala, God provided in a miraculous way once again. I'll admit that at first I was surprised; now I find myself expectant. I have seen way too much to not believe that God will provide for our needs as long as we seek His Kingdom.

Some pastors might be called to be fundraisers; not all of us are. But Jesus does invite us all to be a part of the *missio dei* (the mission of God). He promises to lead us and empower us by His Spirit as we go and bring the message of hope to this broken world. He also promises to take care of our needs.

After two years in Guatemala, the decision was made to build the Buena Vista Sports Academy (BVSA) for boys. The idea had come after much thought and prayer over how to have a long-term impact on a culture that is ravaged by alcoholism and domestic violence. The answer: reach the next generation of men by teaching the boys what it means to be godly men and loving husbands. The premise was to reach the boys in order to bring about lasting change for generations to come.

The story of what God did in the next few months was amazing. To begin, a youth group raised money on their own to help the poor and needy in Guatemala. They then surprised Brock and Kerrie with a gift of $20,000 and said, "Use this however you feel led." Believing this was confirmation for the boys' academy, Brock sent me a manifesto of sorts, which laid-out the vision and the plan for the project.

About a week later while working on the website for the BVSA, Brock heard a knock at the door. The visitor was a man from Buena Vista whom he had never met. The stranger said, "I have some land that I am thinking about selling, and I wanted to see if you might be interested." Brock was perplexed because he and Kerrie had not mentioned the plan to anyone in the area.

Brock decided to go with him to see the land. During their drive to Buena Vista, they ventured toward the community center and the playground they had helped build for the community. This has become the place where many of the kids gather and play. It's also a regular stop for the mission teams that visit. People play soccer and other games with the kids while some people color with them and just love on the little ones.

As it turned out, by God's design, the property was located directly across the street from this area. It couldn't be more perfect—one acre with an incredible view overlooking Guatemala City and beyond. I could only imagine standing there with one of these boys being mentored and trained, telling him that God created him with a plan and purpose in mind for his life. Whatever it is that God puts in his heart, he can do. The sky's the limit!

Soon after, the land was purchased and the dream started to become a reality. With so many confirmations, it was obvious that God was leading this. Brock had also gotten connected with a contractor who was a follower of Jesus. He was willing to do the job basically at cost and to work on the project as money became available. The next step was to get a bid to see how much money would be needed to build it.

The BVSA would consist of a full-size gymnasium with locker rooms, classrooms, and an onsite home. Certainly the cost would be quite a bit more than $3,000 for a 12x12 house. But how much?

We were all a little shocked to hear that the total price would be more than $300,000! In fact, the response of one of the guys who is a faithful supporter of the ministry was, "$300,000! What? Are you crazy?"

It didn't matter. God had done enough to this point to make it clear that this was part of His plan. To not move forward would be disobedience.

When the time came to begin moving dirt and leveling the land, Brock received a call from the contractor to let him know that it would take $9,000 to begin the project. The money wasn't there, so he told him they would have to wait to start. Brock had already planned a trip back the States and was convinced that while there, he would be able to raise the money for the first phase of the project.

God had a different plan. The very next day, Brock received an unexpected email from Theresa who handled the finances for the ministry. She informed him that they had just received a gift from a first-time donor in the amount of $9,000! Once again, God brought confirmation to what He was doing, and so the project began.

I had just returned from Guatemala, so Brock emailed me immediately to tell me what happened. I was so encouraged that I decided to share the story with the people of Journey on Sunday morning. We had been so involved in what was going on in Guatemala that I knew they would be excited and encouraged by what God was doing. Of course, they were amazed at God's provision for the exact amount and at the exact time it was needed.

The next day I was at home with my family when some friends, who had been out-of-town, stopped by our house. We had just finished dinner, so we hung-out and caught up a bit on how their trip was and what was going on in life.

My friend proceeded to share with me some of the struggles he was having. One was with depression. He had begun questioning some things about God, the Bible, and his faith. Although he had been a Christian for a long time, he was wrestling with his faith on a deep level.

Something I've learned along the way is that God appreciates honesty. Doubt, fear and struggle were also part of the lives of many of the people who we would consider heroes of the faith. For this reason, I encouraged my friend to be honest with God but to also reflect upon God's goodness in his life. Particularly, he needed to remember those times when he had experienced God do things that were undeniably His hand at work.

I went on to share some stories from our recent trip to Guatemala. I told him how we saw God work in some amazing ways while we were there. I also shared the story about the BVSA and how God miraculously provided the exact amount of money at the exact time it was needed. With that, my friend started to get a little choked-up. He looked up at me with tears in his eyes and said,

"You know what's crazy about this story?

That was us.

I wrote that check to Brock."

He continued to tell me that the check had actually been sitting in his office for more than a week because he had kept forgetting to mail it. Then one day, he just knew he had to send it.

"I don't know why, but I just felt like I had to mail it that day. So I did." He also explained that while he was struggling with God over the last couple of weeks, he had said to God in one of those quiet moments, "I just need to know that You are here."

Not only was the timing perfect for what was taking place in Guatemala, it was also perfect for him. God showed him in a very real way that He was not only there, but that He was using him to accomplish His purposes. It was as if God was saying, "I am here, and your life matters! You are a part of something much bigger than what you could ever imagine."

Four months later while I was writing this book, the BVSA was well on its way to being built. Money came in from unexpected sources and in unexpected ways. More than three hundred thousand dollars had been given, and the project still had 60 more days before its scheduled completion date.

The stories of how the money had come in were amazing. Rather than steal all the thunder, I'll leave them out to encourage Brock to write his own book. Let me simply say that there was no elaborate fundraising campaign needed. God had something that He wanted to accomplish, and all He needed was someone who was available and willing to believe.

When you read about those who God used in the past, it's easy to forget that these are men and women just like the rest of us. God graciously chose to show us not only their achievements, but their flaws as well. They were real people with real problems. They also served a real God Who had created them with the intent of using them to reflect His glory and to accomplish His purposes on earth.

Consider the words of King David and the apostle Paul:

"For you created my inmost being; you knit me together in my mother's womb. I praise you because I am fearfully and wonderfully made; your works are wonderful, I know that full well. My frame was not hidden from you when I was made in the secret place. When I was woven together in the depths of the earth, your eyes saw my unformed body. All the days ordained for me were written in your book before one of them came to be" (Psalm 139:13-16).

"For we are God's handiwork, created in Christ Jesus to do good works, which God prepared in advance for us to do" (Ephesians 2:10).

He knit you together in your mother's womb. You are His handiwork—a work of art—hand-crafted by Him and for Him.

He created you for certain things.

He has a plan, so you have a purpose.

He is inviting you to simply believe and join Him in what He is doing on the earth.

The world should be a better place because you are alive!

CHAPTER FOURTEEN

Truth or Dare

Our culture has set us up to be people who work our whole life in order to get to a place where we don't have to trust or depend on anyone. For most of us (myself included), simply living in America has kept us from understanding what trusting God really means. Don't get me wrong; I think it's great that we get to experience the blessing of the prosperity of our country.

The problem is that as a result, we've become spoiled (again, myself included). Therefore, we find it difficult when we undergo a small trial or the need to step out by faith into the realm of the unknown. It's as if we're stretched to the limit, wondering how we'll ever make it.

In no way do I want to minimize our battles, but rather help us put them in perspective. We tend to forget that there are people in this world who genuinely don't know if they'll have food to eat the next day. There are those who have seen friends and loved ones maimed and even killed for the same faith we have the freedom to enjoy publicly day-in and day-out. Some of these people treasure mere pages of the Bible because owning a copy of the Bible in their country is nearly impossible.

Do we really know what it means to trust God?

Do you remember the game *Truth or Dare?* You know, the one that we all played when we were kids. This game was how some of us got our first kiss and when others confessed our deepest secrets, such as whether or not we had a crush on another person in the room.

Well, I would like to challenge you to a game of *Truth or Dare*.

As you know, a simple question is posed to an individual. How that person answers the question determines his or her course of action.

So let me ask you..."Truth or Dare?"

If your answer is "truth," then you can continue reading below.

If you're adventuresome, then take the "dare." You can skip the next two pages, and you'll find your dare on the following page.

Let the games begin...

TRUTH

I recently visited the World Vision website. At the very top of its page, I read these words: "Poverty kills 24,000 children a day."

If this is true, then somewhere in the neighborhood of 20 children died of preventable causes during the time it took for you to read the previous page and contemplate the truth or dare question.

Unicef.org reports that we have actually made some strides in helping provide clean drinking water for those in need throughout the world. What's more, for the first time in history, the number of people without access to clean drinking water has fallen below one billion. That's good, but 900 million are still in need. Moreover, Unicef.org tells us that "Two and half billion people are still without access to improved sanitation – including 1.2 billion who have no facilities at all and are forced to engage in the hazardous and demeaning practice of open defecation."

As you let that sink in, also consider the following: "Half the world, nearly 3 billion people, live on less than two dollars a day. The three richest people in the world - Microsoft Chairman Bill Gates, investor Warren Buffett and Mexican telecom mogul Carlos Slim Helú - have more money than the poorest 48 nations combined." [40]

Is the disparity shocking? Well, did you know that if you own a car, then you are richer than 85% of the world? How about the fact that an annual income of $25,000 puts you well into the top 10% of the wealthiest people in the world? In fact, if you're in the United States while reading this book, you're probably considered rich.

[40] Thomas Kostigen for MarketWatch, "Got $2,200? In this world, you're rich," MSN. com, http://articles.moneycentral.msn.com/News/StudyRevealsOverwhelming WealthGap.aspx, 22 June 2011.

Although some of the statistics on poverty are appalling, the reality is that there is enough food and resources in the world today to take care of all of us who live on the earth.

So what is the real problem here?

Have you ever thought about the countless number of people who live and die in poverty each day? Have you considered that your favorite gourmet coffee drink costs more than most people earn in a day's wages? Has the thought of a starving child ever crossed your mind during an evening meal?

I know you only signed-up for the "truth" part of the game, so let me stop here. Furthermore, I'm going to make it incredibly easy. You don't have to spill your guts or tell any of your deep, dark secrets. You just have to answer one simple "yes" or "no" question. What happens after that is up to you.

A man named John, who was one of Jesus' best friends, made the following statement:

"If anyone has material possessions and sees a brother or sister in need but has no pity on them, how can the love of God be in that person?" (1 John 3:17).

So here is your "Truth" question:

Is the love of God in you?

If so, then what will you do about it?

DARE

I dare you to do the following:

Go to www.globalrichlist.com and answer one quick question. Then when you're finished, pray this prayer found in Proverbs:

"O God, I beg two favors from you; let me have them before I die. First, help me never to tell a lie. Second, *give me neither poverty nor riches!* Give me just enough to satisfy my needs. For if I grow rich, I may deny you and say, 'Who is the Lord?' And if I am too poor, I may steal and thus insult God's holy name" (Proverbs 30:7-9 NLT).

Surprised by your ranking?

Scared to pray the prayer?

Me too...

God, help us to trust You more as we learn what it means to give ourselves away, just as You did for each of us.

"For you know the grace of our Lord Jesus Christ, that though He was rich, yet for your sake He became poor, so that you by His poverty might become rich" (2 Corinthians 8:9 ESV).

CHAPTER FIFTEEN

Re:Think Church

We need to stop giving people excuses not to believe in God. You've probably heard the expression 'I believe in God, just not organized religion'. I don't think people would say that if the church truly lived like we are called to live.[41]
---Francis Chan

We're living in a time when it's paramount for us to understand that the New Testament Church has nothing to do with buildings, denominations, institutions or programs. Along with God's presence, only one other factor is necessary in order to have a true expression of God's Church, and that's people. The Church is made up of those who name Jesus as their Savior and submit to Him as Lord. Therefore, I believe the time has come to lay all of our preconceived ideas and notions on the altar and begin to rethink Church.

As a point of clarification, I'm not saying that buildings, denominations, programs, etc. do not have a place in the scope of how the church is expressed. I'm merely noting the fact that these are not Biblically-mandated components of the church; therefore they're non-essentials when defining church. That being said, God has seemingly given us a lot of latitude on how a local expression of the church might look and function.

This means that a mega-church of 10,000 and a house church of 10 can both be legitimate expressions of God's Church and can equally glorify Him. This means that Baptists, Presbyterians and Char-

[41] Francis Chan, *Crazy Love: Overwhelmed by a Relentless God,* (Colorado Springs: David C. Cook, 2008), 21.

ismatics alike can be used by God to accomplish His purposes. This also means less traditional and new expressions of the church can be legitimate as well.

The expression of church may be very different from place to place. Apparently though, some key components must be present in order to be true to what we see modeled by Jesus, the apostles and the early Church. For instance, the very essence of Christ's ministry was relational. The apostles were His friends, and His ministry often took place in a relational context. This was passed onto the early Church as they broke bread together in their homes and at times shared their possessions. With this in mind, if the church of today wants to continue to function the way Jesus intended, then it must also be relational.

Also when I read the New Testament and particularly the words of Jesus, I'm led to believe that the foundation of the Church is love. Jesus put it this way: "'Love the Lord your God with all your heart and with all your soul and with all your mind. This is the first and greatest commandment. And the second is like it: "Love your neighbor as yourself." All the Law and the Prophets hang on these two commandments.'"[42] According to Jesus, this was the most important command His followers needed to understand.

Maybe it's really all about this one thing.

Love.

Jesus did more than just speak these words; He lived them. Not only was His life the perfect example of love, His incarnation screams of His love for mankind. Jesus stepped out of heaven and into our world because He loved us. Have you given that much thought? He willingly left His place in heaven, knowing full well that He would be rejected, brutally and horrifically beaten and ultimately crucified by those He created.

He sacrificed everything to show us this one thing.

Love.

Love must be the foundation of all ministry that takes place in the

---

[42] Matthew 22:37-40.

name of Jesus. For a person to be a part of His Church, His love must first be in that person.

In 1 Peter 4:8, we're told that love covers a multitude of sins. In one single act of love, all of the sin that has been committed and ever will be committed was paid in full. "You see, at just the right time, when we were still powerless, Christ died for the ungodly. Very rarely will anyone die for a righteous person, though for a good person someone might possibly dare to die. But God demonstrates His own love for us in this: While we were still sinners, Christ died for us" (Romans 5:6-8).

What an incredible display of love.

Jesus didn't do this just for good people. He willingly died for all people. For the pastor, priest, pimp and prostitute, Jesus gave His life. Because He loved us, and for His glory, He died and rose to gain life for any and all who would believe.

There is no greater gift that one can give. However, a gift must first be received for a person to truly benefit from it. "He came to that which was His own, but His own did not receive Him. Yet to all who received Him, to those who believed in His name, He gave the right to become children of God" (John 1:11-12).

You have been given a gift. But you must receive it.

The choice is yours.

You have been invited into a beautiful relationship. Our perfect Father wants you as a son or daughter.

Religion is not what He desires.

He wants your heart.

He wants you.

Yes, you.

He gave His only Son so that we all might become sons and daughters. "For God so loved the world that He gave His one and only Son, that whoever believes in Him shall not perish but have eternal life. For God did not send his Son into the world to condemn the world, but to save the world through Him. Whoever believes in Him is not condemned, but whoever does not believe stands condemned already because he has not believed in the name of God's one and only Son" (John 3:16-18).

The Father sent the Son to remove our condemnation.[43] Why would God do such a thing? What would God want from those who would receive such a gift? What would be the one thing that would mark such people—His Church?

Love.

So, what does love look like?

Love looks like a person who sees a woman on the side of the road with her two children and feels compelled to stop. So they do.

Love looks like a guy who decides to take blankets downtown to offer to those on the streets on a cold winter night.

Love looks like a group of people who decide that it's more important to build houses for those living in third-world abject poverty than it is to invest in a bigger building for their growing church.

Love looks like a wife and mother who makes it her mission to see slavery abolished in her lifetime.

Love looks like someone who gives anonymously to the couple who is out of work during economically-challenging times.

Love looks like those who don't give up on the drug addict who continues to fall time-and-time-again but expresses a desire to be free.

Love looks like a person who leaves the comforts of living in America in order to serve those who are living in utter poverty in the third world.

Love looks like people who choose to die to themselves, doing these kinds of things, expecting nothing in return.

"Greater love has no one than this, that he lay down his life for his friends" (John 15:13).

Love looks like Jesus.

The Church should look like Jesus as well.

---

[43] Romans 8:1.

We are the Church.

When we look at the life of Jesus, we see that His love is very different from ours. Rarely do we love others without expecting anything in return. Even if it's a simple "thank you," we expect some reciprocation for our love. Jesus loved people. Period. He loved with no strings attached. He expressed love to those who had no ability to repay Him. He loved them, and in doing so, gave us the perfect example of God's love for us.

What if we decided to love like Jesus did, with no strings attached?

How would people respond?

Would it change things?

Many of those outside the church are suspicious, and rightfully so. They think Christians have some kind of agenda behind everything they do. They think they're either after their money, or they're trying to change them in some way. That's why so many people keep Christians at arm's length.

It reminds me of the feelings I get when I visit a used car lot. I do everything I can to let the car salesman know that I'm not buying anything and that I would prefer to be left alone. I've heard the spiel and really don't want to be pestered. My thoughts are, "Just let me do my thing, and when I'm ready, I'll come and find you."

I think a lot of people are like this when it comes to their spirituality. They might be seeking spiritually, but they really don't want some "know-it-all" trying to sell them something. To them, these individuals obviously have an agenda, and they would rather seek at their own pace. When the time is right, they'll come looking and asking questions, but they need their space.

People don't like to feel manipulated, and most can tell when you have some sort of agenda. Jesus never made people feel that way, so why should we? When you show love to a person with no hidden plan, you are then showing them God's love.

Showing love with no strings attached is disarming.

LOVE BROKE THROUGH

Caesar and Lillian Gomez are a sweet young Guatemalan couple with a beautiful little girl named Stefani. I came to know them through the "12x12 Love Project" since they were one of the original 12 families to receive a home.

When homes are given to families, there are no expectations of the family and literally no strings attached. The gift is given in the name of Jesus, and relationships are formed during and after the construction period. We leave it up to God to do the rest, and He often does some cool stuff in the process, like what we saw with the Gomez family.

I had the privilege of being there when this couple was presented with the keys to their new home. Seeing the excitement and joy that filled everyone present was an awesome experience. When we gave them the keys, we took time to pray for them and let them know that this was a gift from God; we were only the messengers used to deliver it. The moment was very emotional and was only heightened when Caesar announced that he wanted to know this Jesus Who had blessed his family so abundantly. Lillian wasn't ready to make such a commitment. But through her tears, she thanked us and thanked God and merely asked us to pray for her.

When I returned home, I shared the story with the people at Journey. Everyone was familiar with Caesar and Lillian because weeks earlier, we had showed pictures of their family and told their story during one of our gatherings. Many people had been praying for this young couple. You could imagine how excited they were to hear about Caesar's new-found faith.

I later found out that there was one woman who was particularly moved by it all. After hearing the story, a single mom in our spiritual community took it upon herself to contact the Johnsons. She told them that she felt impressed to help the family and asked if there was anything they needed. Brock told her about some of the household needs, so she sent him $150 so that Caesar's family could purchase a table and chairs as well as a few other items for their home.

A week or so later, Brock and his family stopped by to visit Caesar and Lillian who were still very excited and thankful for their new home. As the Johnsons were about to leave, Brock remembered to tell them about the donation that was given to help them buy some of the furniture they needed. Immediately, Lillian began sobbing. Brock wondered if he had done something wrong. Did he make a cultural error, or could his "Spanglish" have failed him terribly in some way?

Through her tears, Lillian asked why God continued to do this. "Why does He keep blessing me? I am such a bad person, I don't deserve this," she said.

At that point, Brock let Lillian know that she wasn't alone. "The reality is that we are all sinful, and none of us deserves God's love. That's the good news expressed to us in Jesus."

Lillian broke.

She gave her heart to this Jesus Who had loved her unconditionally, not only through His death on the cross, but through the tangible gifts of His followers as well.

Love.

The true Church of Jesus is an unstoppable force driven by His love for a world that's broken, hurting and in need of reconciliation and restoration. If we viewed those outside the Church the way Jesus did, I believe things would be different. Jesus never showed anything but love to those who were far from the Father. As we have seen, He reserved His harshest words for the religious people who thought they had it all together and considered themselves better than others.

Jesus' actions and words lead me to believe that the church has a lot to learn when it comes to loving as He did. While Jesus spoke truth and never once encouraged sin, He also never came off angry toward those who were the farthest from God. He was comfortable moving in their circles, and many of them were drawn to Him. This infuriated the religious people of His time, causing them to label Him a drunkard, glutton and a friend of sinners.[44]

If we are to follow Jesus and be like Him, I would think that we

---

[44] Luke 7:34.

should see a similar response. Many on the outside who are far from God should be drawn to us. And if we're living purposefully in this world, we should also see the same kind of backlash from legalistic religious people that Jesus did. As someone once said, "If we aren't ticking-off religious people on a regular basis, then we probably aren't living like Jesus."

Jesus didn't seem swayed by popular opinion or the expectations of religious people in His day. He was motivated to do the will of the Father, and that meant God's Kingdom took precedent over this earthly kingdom. He was OK with offending people when necessary, and He always had the Kingdom of God as His first priority. This may be the most glaring difference between Jesus' ministry and that of most local churches today.

What takes priority in the church today?

Is it that which brings the greatest benefit to God's Kingdom, or is it whatever brings the greatest benefit to "our" ministry? Jesus didn't seem too concerned with building a ministry or a following. He was more concerned with doing what was right and bringing glory to the Father. Maybe we would do well to take note of this.

The more the church has become program-driven and institutionalized, the more we have found ourselves needing to be concerned with sustaining "it," rather than having God's Kingdom as our first priority. I may not agree totally with those who say, "small is the new big" when it comes to church; nevertheless, I do think there's something to be said for the simple church model that's more easily sustained and reproducible.

In its purest form, church is really not that complex. It's a gathered group of believers who are seeking first God's Kingdom in this world. They love God with all their heart, and they love their neighbors as they do their own lives. They believe the Bible to be true and look to it for guidance on how to function and display God's Kingdom here on earth. They see each person as a valuable member. They encourage one another to use their God-given gifts and talents to share the good news of the gospel as they share their lives with others.

When the church looks and operates like this, it is beautiful. There are no superstars and no agendas other than God's. There is no territory to defend and no competition necessary. It doesn't take a million-dollar budget to sustain, and it shows love to any and all who come in contact with it. This is a church that's for all people. This is the Church that Jesus promised He would build and that nothing, not even the gates of hades, could prevail against it. [45]

So, if you're on the outside looking in, I would encourage you to not give up on Jesus or His Church. If you have been burned and are considering walking away for good, I urge you to give God and His Church one more chance. Maybe you're a leader of a more traditional American expression of church, and you're feeling the need for change. Know that you're not alone and that God is stirring the hearts of many like yourself.

You will never know what awaits you unless you are willing to re-think Church.

I had coffee with a friend of mine a few weeks ago. He told me that after much prayer and soul searching, he and his wife had come to the conclusion that they have way more than what they need. They have always been people who give, but they started feeling like much of what they had been giving in the past was out of excess.

They began to wonder what it would be like if they gave themselves a salary cap, so to speak. They would live off of a certain amount, and then anything that came in after that, they would give away. My friend does pretty well, but he doesn't make crazy money. Recently he told me that he wrote his first check for those in need. When the money actually left his back account, he said he "felt it," but he also said, "It felt good."

I have another friend who has been a part of our spiritual community since day-one. He was there for the cookouts and Bible studies in our home, and he has been a leader in the church ever since. He and his wife have recently decided that God was calling their family to be

[45]Matthew 16:18.

full time missionaries to Guatemala. He's the last guy who I would have ever thought would do something like that. By the time you read this, they will be living in Guatemala, showing the love of Jesus to people as they work with the "12x12 Love Project."

A few months back, I had a guy come and tell me that he felt like God wanted him to give his pristine 1975 Corvette Stingray to the church so that it could be sold and used for one of our "crazy love" projects.

Two other good friends have recently approached me to let me know that they feel God is leading them to take a year to go and serve Jesus on the mission field in Guatemala.

Today after our church gathering, a young couple told me they felt like God was calling them to move to Haiti. They're now beginning to pray and plan accordingly. They hope to go sometime in the next three years.

I had a meeting with another couple last week who believe that God wants them to start a homeless shelter here in Jacksonville to help meet the needs of those on the streets.

Honestly, I have no idea what's going to happen in each of the situations I've mentioned. All I know is that God's people are beginning to dream, and with God, all things are possible.

I think it's time for more people to begin to dream, to dream that "church" as we know it and have known it for years can be different. It can be more about God and His purposes and not about men and their accomplishments. I think it's time to begin to dream that the church can get back to its Biblical roots, even in a country where culture moves people toward self-indulgence and self-centered living.

The good news is that those on the outside are not the only ones who recognize the need for change. There are people on the inside who are feeling unrest and are searching for something more. In addition, I have recently found myself talking to more and more pastors who realize that the church is in desperate need of some type of reformation.

Whether we refer to it as reformation or revival, I think many of us would agree that there is a great need for change within the church today. Throughout history, this sort of change has occurred when God's people have humbled themselves and prayed. After seeking God through prayer and being led by His Spirit, those who God is calling to be catalysts of this movement will then need to take bold steps of faith.

There is a fresh wind blowing through the church today. My hope and prayer are that you will join God in what He is doing to make His name great in this country and throughout the world.

As I have said throughout the course of this book, I am far from having it all figured out. All I know is that God has me on a journey of rediscovery when it comes to His Church and how it's to function in this world. The ride has been incredible to this point. God has amazed me by His grace and has humbled me when I've seen Him do miraculous things around me. To be able to serve Him and join Him in what He is doing to accomplish His purposes here on the earth is an incredible privilege.

I agree with Mother Teresa who said, "I alone cannot change the world, but I can cast a stone across the waters to create many ripples."

What if we were all willing to cast our stones? What kind of ripples would we make if we believed that God had a purpose in creating us and then we sought to join Him in His purposes? What if we made it our mission to love God first with all our heart, soul, mind and strength and to then show that same love to those who are in need all around us?

What difference would it make?

Only God knows.

And I would say that the world and the church

are literally dying to know.

LOVE.

Changing lives... One house at a time!